SMELL YOUR REFLECTIONS

ON THE SOUL'S MEANINGFUL SCENT IMAGES

Brian Falk

Smell Your Reflections:
On the Soul's Meaningful Scent Images

A dissertation submitted
by

Brian Falk

to
Pacifica Graduate Institute

in partial fulfillment of
the requirements for the
degree of

Doctor in Philosophy in
Depth Psychology

with emphasis in
Somatic Studies

This dissertation has been
accepted for the faculty of
Pacifica Graduate Institute by:

Dr. Jennifer Selig, Chair

Dr. Alan Kilpatrick, Reader

Dr. Hans Rindisbacher, External Reader

Manuscript approved: APRIL 26, 2018

Copyright 2018

Brian Falk

ISBN: 978-1728936222

Abstract
Smell Your Reflections:
On the Soul's Meaningful Scent Images
by
Brian Falk

This research investigates the role of meaningful aromas through a hermeneutical intersection of the natural sciences, philosophy, and depth psychology. Part 1 analyzes how fragrances can be constructed as psychic images. Following Jung, perceptual images are differentiated from memory images. Four qualities necessary for the formation of scent images are then identified: evocative, idiosyncratic, emotional, and adherence. Part 2 discusses more specifically the factors involved in the formation of meaningful aromas. Beginning with the need for adequate olfactory language, the role of breath, aesthetics, memory, and the imagination, placed within the context of a particular scent experience are outlined. The final part of the research explores the psyche's reflective process regarding meaningful scent images and the psychological implications derived from this experience. Following the work of Hillman and Berry, two styles of reflection are proposed: zooming in and zooming out. The body's role in the reflective process and the self-knowledge derived from attending to somatic sensations is then discussed. The findings reveal that meaningful scent images could be harnessed to improve psychological health by providing emotional fulfillment, a stronger sense of identity, and greater self-knowledge. The results suggest that scent imagery could be used in clinical applications to foster self-esteem and strengthening one's sense of life continuity.

ACKNOWLEDGEMENTS

I want to thank my father, whose incessant sniffing and attention to aromas sparked my own scent obsession. I thank my large family, especially my mother and sister, for their support, love, and encouragement to be my weird and offbeat self. Deep gratitude to Bridget for helping me wrestle with the most challenging psychological ideas, for her clarity of thought and sharp editing skills, and for nudging me forward when I felt most defeated. I wish to thank my committee for their guidance and enthusiasm in my project and for teaching me to be a better writer. I also would like to thank my classmates, whose friendship, passion, and wisdom keeps the heart-fire alive. Finally, I want to thank the world of aromas for adding a rich texture throughout my life.

Table of Contents

With some exceptions, the style used throughout this dissertation is in accordance with the *Publication Manual of the American Psychological Association* (6th Edition, 2009), and *Pacifica Graduate Institute's Dissertation Handbook* (2017-18).

Chapter 1

INTRODUCTION

The morning wind spreads its fresh smell
We must get up and take that in,
that wind that lets us live
Breathe before it's gone
~Rumi, The Essential Rumi

Helen Keller called smell the "fallen angel" among
the senses and pondered why it "does not hold the high
position it deserves among its sisters" (2009, p. 26). While
it is true that compared to vision and audition, olfaction is
less researched and appears less important, it has
nonetheless been investigated in a variety of fields and
disciplines. Ranging from the natural sciences of
chemistry, physics, and biology, to the humanities fields
of anthropology and psychology, olfaction and its
influence have not been completely neglected.

The sense of smell is one way the human psyche
(defined below) experiences itself and the world.
Although it is common knowledge that scents are closely
tied to memories and emotions, the idea that scent can be a
psychic image is seldom discussed, even in the field of
depth psychology. Furthermore, even though the
prominent psychologist C.G. Jung (1875-1961) states that
"the psyche consists essentially of images" (1928/1969, p.
325), the idea of scent being an image has not been
directly examined for its psychological implications. My
research will begin by first defining and then examining

the nature of psychic images, followed by making a case for understanding scent as a psychic image.

A primary assumption in depth psychology is that psychic images have the function of making meaning. The question that follows this assumption is thus: if an aroma can qualify as a psychic image, can scent as image invoke a feeling of meaningfulness? In order to answer this question, I must investigate the literature in the field of depth psychology as well as olfactory research in the natural sciences.

Because psychological ideas are strengthened by ideas from other disciplines, this dissertation will enrich the understanding of olfaction in the natural sciences by offering a deeper soul-perspective, and in return infuse the broad field of depth psychology with a greater appreciation of scent. This combining of disciplines will constitute an interdisciplinary approach that involves depth psychology and the natural sciences, with the intention of bringing the two together, perhaps even dissolving some boundaries. I will also attempt to promote new theoretical directions, seeking to make a contribution to both fields. I am hopeful that through a careful investigation of psychological and scientific texts, new perspectives will be generated.

Definition of Terms

The following terms will be used frequently throughout this study and therefore require the clearest definitions possible. These terms are also foundational for the main ideas to be investigated. Many of the terms have, of course, different definitions in a variety of contexts. In this section I have attempted to keep the definitions as fundamental as possible. A more comprehensive discussion of these terms will be explored in the literature review section of chapter two.

Psyche and Soul

According to psychologist Bruno Bettelheim (1982), the word *psyche* can be traced back to ancient Greece and is typically translated as *soul* (p. 73). The founder of psychoanalysis, Sigmund Freud (1856-1939), translated psyche into the German word *seele* (as cited in Bettelheim, 1982), which in English means soul. In most of Freud's writings he used seele, as opposed to *geist*, which means "mind," or "intellect" (as cited in Bettelheim, 1982, p. 76). In this dissertation I will use psyche and soul interchangeably, and, like Freud, use these terms as opposed to mind or intellect.

Unfortunately, soul and psyche have a multitude of meanings in today's American culture. To use these words, therefore, presents some difficulties if they are not clearly defined. *Psychology* is typically defined as the study of the mind, so it is logical to equate the word psyche with mind or intellect. The American edition of the *Oxford Dictionary and Thesaurus* (1997) defines the word psychology as the "scientific study of the human mind" (Psychology, p. 641). Yet they define the word psyche more inclusively: "1. Soul; spirit. 2. Mind" (Psyche, p. 641). The definition of soul is even more inclusive, the *Oxford Dictionary* listing six different meanings: "1. Spiritual or immaterial part of a human being, often regarded as immortal. 2. Moral or emotional or intellectual nature of a person or animal. 3. Personification or pattern of something. 4. An individual. 5. Animating or essential part. 6. African-American culture, music, etc." (Soul, p. 762).

In the context of this dissertation I wish to clarify what I mean by psyche and soul. I will not use soul in the common religious or spiritual sense, taken to be immortal, or having connotations of an afterlife or previous incarnations. Nor will I be using soul in a metaphysical or supernatural context. When I use the word soul, I am not referring to a particular entity, nor a thing that can be pinned down, measured, fully grasped, or studied like neurons in the brain. The paradox here is that soul and psyche cannot be fully defined or quantified, for soul is ambiguous, fluid, deeply hidden, intangible, and complex (Coppin & Nelson, 2005, pp. 42-86); yet, those qualities are essentially what make us human.

I also will not equate psyche specifically with the intellect or mind; although psyche, as I define it, does make use of the intellect and cannot be separated from it. Any attempt to study or define the innermost essence of human beings through the scientific lens, looking at behavior, brain states, or physiology—what can be measured or observed from the outside—is inadequate to defining soul.

I will thus define soul and psyche to mean one's innermost being or character. This innermost being includes both our conscious and our unconscious life, comprising our thoughts, feelings, emotions, symptoms, memories, habits, dreams, and the imagination. I would like to follow Bettelheim's (1982) train of thought, with which I imagine Freud and Jung would both agree, namely, that soul is an overarching, comprehensive concept or metaphor. However, its connotations of interiority and deep feeling keep the meaning closer to our common human experience, which mind or intellect does not. Even though it is common to "view our intellectual life separate or even opposed to our emotional life" (p. 71), feelings and emotions are key descriptive qualities of soul as used in this dissertation.

Image

My definition of the word *image* is in keeping with Jung and archetypal psychologist James Hillman (1926-2011). The term image will be used to mean the very substance of the psyche. "The psyche consists essentially of images," writes Jung (1928/1969, p. 325). Further, "what appears to us as immediate reality consists of carefully processed images...we live immediately only in a world of images" (1933/1969b, p. 384). Thus, image will not refer merely to a visual object or a mental picture, but rather is to be understood in a broader perspective. "Even physical pain," observes Jung, "is a psychic image which I experience; my sense impressions...are psychic images, and these alone constitute my immediate objects of my consciousness" (1933/1969a, p. 353). To this Hillman adds, "An image cannot be something only set before my eyeballs, or even before my mind's eye, since it is also something into which I enter and by which I am embraced. Images hold us; we can be in the grip of an image" (1978, p. 159). Hillman offers an example: "A dream is an entire image, no matter how fragmentary" (1977, p. 66), and "is complete just as it presents itself" (1977, p. 68). Therefore, an image may present itself as a melody, color, smell, feeling tone, or movement.

6

Meaning and Meaningful

Most people will agree that there are numerous philosophical and linguistic interpretations on how meaning occurs. For the sake of simplicity, I would like to use the ideas of Edward Edinger, a student of Jung, to characterize the word *meaning* in this dissertation. Edinger (1992) differentiates two basic usages of meaning: objective and subjective. On the one hand, abstract, objective knowledge conveyed by a sign or representation is a token of meaning that stands for a known entity. On the other hand, subjective meaning does not refer to abstract knowledge, but rather to a psychological state that can affirm life (pp. 108-109). It is the subjective type of meaning that I will refer to in the context of this dissertation. A key distinction, explains Edinger, between objective and subjective meaning is that the latter is filled with emotion, sometimes described as "deeply moving," and is always unique and particular to the individual (p. 108). In other words, meaning will be described as personal, emotional, and embodied. I add the characteristic *embodied* to Edinger's definition to emphasize that subjective meaning has a bodily component that provides important information to the individual in the form of physiological sensations. *Embodied meaning* is contrasted with the view taken by analytic and formalist philosophy, where meaning is tied to language and tends to be disembodied, literal, abstract, and objective (Lakoff & Johnson, 1999, pp. 440-443).

The word *meaningful* will be used in a way similar to the subjective meaning just mentioned. It refers to something that is full of meaning, significant, important, serious, and deep.

Sensation and Perception

The words *sensation* and *perception* are closely related but need to be differentiated in the context of this study. Whereas sensation will be used to mean a feeling in one's body detected by the senses (*Oxford Dictionary*, 1997), perception will be used to describe the process of sensations reaching parts of the brain and nervous system that then organize, translate, and interpret the sensory information (Schacter, Gilbert, Wegner, & Nock, 2015, p. 96). Perception can thus give meaning to sensations through the context of emotions, memories, images, and past experiences.

Odorants

Odorants are the distal or external olfactory stimuli from which molecules emanate. The words *odor* and *smell* refer to odor sensory experience. Thus, the sensation of odor is the result of stimulation by an odorant (Engen, 1982, p. 2). In this dissertation, I will use a broad psychological definition of the sense of smell, where odor and smell refer to both the proximal, resulting psychological and physiological response and the distal source. Smell will therefore be used as both noun and verb. The words odor, *scent, fragrance,* and *aroma* will be used as synonyms for smell as a noun. The adjectives *fragrant, aromatic,* and *odoriferous* will also be used synonymously for smell. The word *perfume* will only be used to refer to alcohol-based or fermented liquid mixtures. *Olfaction* as a noun will be largely synonymous

8

with, and as a more scientific term than, the *sense of smell*, as well as the adjective *olfactory*, a scientific term that relates to the sense of smell.

Psychophysics

The terms *psychophysics* or *psychophysical* will be used to describe the relation between external, physical stimulation and internal experience, between body and mind. Here, *psycho-* refers to sensory or experienced subjective magnitude, like loudness or odor intensity, while *physical* refers to sounds, pressure, or concentration (Engen, 1982, p. 5). Take for instance, air pollution. One would begin with the environmental stimulus, such as certain chemical pollutants in the air, then follow their course from the receptors in the nose and olfactory bulb to higher centers in the brain. It is at this point that the brain and mind/psyche come together to form a subjective evaluation of air pollution. This latter part of the process accounts for different people's wide range of responses to the same stimulus.

Soma and Somatics

Consistent with philosopher Thomas Hanna's (1995) definitions, this dissertation will occasionally use the words *soma* and *somatic* to be differentiated from the word *body*. Soma will be used to refer to a body as perceived from within by first-person perception, using one's own proprioceptive senses. This is contrasted with a human body that is viewed from an outside, third-person perspective, as in the case of physiology. Body and soma are equivalent in physical reality but are categorically distinct as observed phenomena and perceived experience (pp. 341-42).

Odor Memory

Odor-evoked memories are autobiographical memories and associations that are triggered by odors (Herz, 2016, p. 1). Odor-evoked memories can be either explicit (conscious) or implicit (unconscious). Long-term odor-evoked memory is different than *sensory memory*, which is a memory of an earlier sensation compared with the one experienced in the present moment. Sensory memory serves to monitor an unfamiliar or familiar odor in a certain environmental context within a relatively short time frame (typically in less than one second). Sensory memory is an inherent factor in all psychophysical experience (Engen, 1991, p. 29), whereas long-term odor-evoked memory occurs primarily in the psyche. I will also take into account memories of particular odors themselves, where the scent is not only a trigger of memory but as an object of perception.

Relevance of the Topic for Depth Psychology

In order to generate new perspectives, we must first collect and present what is already known; we must have a starting place. Since the essential topic of this dissertation is the meaning of scents for the human soul, our starting point is in depth psychology, which places "the soul at the center of human concerns," and focuses on studying and reporting human experience (Coppin & Nelson, 2005, p. 21). Thus, in an attempt to generate a new perspective this dissertation embarks on a soul-centered research approach.

Depth psychology grounds itself in the fundamental reality of the psyche, and "draws one beneath the surface of thought, word, and action to the inclinations and impulses of the soul they are rooted in" (Coppin & Nelson, 2005, p. 42). Depth psychology pays attention to both the seen and the unseen, the known and the unknown, and both surface and depth of all phenomena. It gathers and includes all that is marginalized, unacknowledged, forgotten, dismissed, neglected, and buried. This research, therefore, aims to find qualities about scents and olfactory experiences that are not yet known, offer new perspectives, or make connections that have yet to be linked.

One of the pioneers of the psychological study of olfaction, Trygg Engen (1926-2009), suggests in, *The Perception of Odors* (1982), that the sense of smell has a unique place among the senses in that it is the subtlest and the most transitory. As a scientist, Engen admits that olfaction is the most difficult sense to quantify, categorize, or fully understand scientifically. This is yet another reason why the primary lens of my research will be through depth psychology and not, for instance, neuroscience or physiology. Depth psychology is a field that recognizes the variable, complex, and unclear expressions of psychic experience, and whose approach is more appropriate for my research study.

Depth psychology also embraces different epistemologies and respects many ways of knowing. "People know what they know through sensation, intuition, and imagination working in concert with reason"

(Coppin & Nelson, 2005, p. 51). Olfaction falls under the realm of sensation as a way of knowing, although this sense is often given less respect or credibility as a means of knowing compared with vision or audition. I would add to the quote above that through our feelings, we also know the emotions in our soma. The connection between scent and emotion is well established and may offer a new perspective as a meaningful epistemology.

Thus far I have made the case for grounding this dissertation in depth psychology for the purposes of investigating scents as psychic images and exploring what they might mean for the soul. I chose the field of depth psychology for its psyche-centered approach to research, its respect for multiple ways of knowing, and its strength in creating a multimodal approach to knowledge.

On the one hand, it is not surprising that the natural sciences have stopped short in investigating the meaning of scents to the soul. After all, it is not the goal of biology, chemistry, or physics to probe into the depth of a human's imagination and dreams, looking for profound idiosyncratic meaning. For this we have depth psychology and its approaches to carry the thrust of this dissertation, informing the natural sciences in ways generally not considered or even imagined.

On the other hand, it is somewhat surprising that the field of depth psychology so far has paid scant attention to aromas, the sense of smell, and their relationship to the psyche. Although perhaps not too surprising considering how relatively new the field is, having just arisen at the end of the 19th century. Further, there is a wide range of other ideas and topics that have attracted and consumed scholars and clinicians' attention, thereby easily pushing aside scents and olfaction. Another explanation could be that aromas are too ambiguous, short-lived, and fleeting. It is possible that a scent's transient nature leaves even the depth psychologist and phenomenologist with nothing to grasp onto, gone before it is truly recognized. Or scents simply may not be meaningful to some researchers. Nevertheless, the omission of anything related to olfaction, smell, aromas, etc. from the literature in the field of depth psychology is perplexing.

There are a few examples that highlight this point. The first is the pre-eminent philosopher of the body, Maurice Merleau-Ponty (1908-1961), whose famous work, *Phenomenology of Perception* (1945/2012), greatly contributed to the field of depth psychology and has been influential across many academic disciplines. It would seem logical to find a philosophical perspective on olfaction in his masterpiece. *Phenomenology of Perception* is close to five hundred pages, yet, according to the index (pp. 593-605), there are 46 entries on vision and 65 entries on gaze, while the number of entries on smell, scent, and olfaction is zero. The French are historically and famously known for their love of cuisine, which includes the aromas of delicious food, so where are Merleau-Ponty's references to smell?

Another example is the philosopher and ecologist David Abram who produced a beautiful work entitled, *The Spell of the Sensuous* (1996). However, the 275 pages of his book, richly packed with descriptions of our senses, contain only one entry in the index on smell (or related words such as aroma, odor, etc.). There are a few brief descriptions of smell sprinkled throughout the book, such as: "Even our noses seemed to come awake, the fresh smells from the ocean somehow more vibrant and salty" (p. 63), and "The encounter is influenced, as well, by the fresh smell of the autumn wind, and even by the taste of an apple that still lingers on my tongue" (p. 60). It is as if Abram intuits the importance of smells, but glosses over the details, hurrying on to other senses, and choosing trite and generic descriptions like "fresh, salty ocean" and "fresh autumn wind."

A further example is in the voluminous published works of Jung where there is hardly a trace of direct attention to the sense of smell. In his theory of the psychological types (first published in 1921), Jung writes thoughtfully of the sensation type personality and the process of perception. Although the body and soma were not the primary focus of Jung's work, he did devote lengthy chapters on the senses in general, notably in Collected Works 6. Yet the co-founder of depth psychology also left aromas to the wind.

The other co-founder, Sigmund Freud (1930/2010), did touch upon the sense of smell, albeit through an anthropological and biological lens. "In spite of the undeniable diminution in the importance of olfactory stimuli, there exists even in Europe races who prize highly as aphrodisiacs the strong genital odours so objectionable to us and who will not renounce them," and "In spite of all man's evolutionary progress the smell of his own excretions is scarcely disagreeable to him" (pp. 66-78). His emphasis was less on the sense of smell directly and what it may mean to the individual, and more on the evolution of culture from a sexual and biological standpoint. On this last point I must note that Freud was influenced by his physician friend, Wilhelm Fliess, an ear and nose specialist who theorized a correspondence between the nasal mucosa and the genital organs (Ellenberger, 1970, p. 444). Fliess' ideas may have led Freud to view the repression of olfactory pleasure, along with man's upright stance, as a necessary stage in humanity's move toward more "civilized" living. "Repression of smell meant the repression of wild sexual impulses and their redirection to more refined behavior" (Gilbert, 2008, p. 58). Consequently, Freud came to see olfaction as a primitive and obsolete sense, no longer needed for modern man. Freud's complete dismissal of even the practical side of olfaction may seem radical but perhaps understandable because, as Gilbert hypothesizes, "Freud suffered from hyposmia…a clinically impaired sense of smell" (p. 60). In any case, Freud published little on the topic of olfaction, thus minimally contributing to the psychology of scent.

The one exception of a scholar who deals with the sense of smell from a depth psychological perspective is James Hillman. Most notably, Hillman's (1979a) essay, "Image Sense," touches upon scent characteristics: "Smells cannot stand alone. They must be linked to an image: rose-odor, toast-scent, refinery-stench" (p. 140). Yet Hillman writes about the sense of smell and aromas mostly as metaphor and uses analogies to explain psychological ideas, rather than pondering scents and their effects directly. "Smelling is the best sense analogy for imagining…if we want to understand an image for itself, we must smell it out. We need a good nose for differences" (p. 140). In some writings he does, however, connect aromas with spirit and emotions. "When we smell something, we are taking in its spirit, so it is just as well to know what we are smelling" (p. 187). In his first published book, *Emotion*, Hillman (1960) claims that, "emotion stirred by scent is particularly powerful because scent is the privileged manifestation of spirit…each object has its own 'air,' its own 'smell,' or affective quality which is its spirit" (p. 235). Thus, although Hillman as a depth psychologist does write about scents, it is still minimal compared to the rest of his extensive published works.

Lastly, there is one other author whose work is written from a depth psychological perspective and thus will be invaluable for my research. Helen Keller (1880-1968) was not a depth psychologist or a scientist, yet her writings reflect a quintessential display of a soul-centered perspective. Both blind and deaf, her sense of smell was extremely important for her ability to navigate the environment. Yet beyond the practical necessities of the sense of smell, Keller's intelligent, sharp, and poetic mind was deeply sourced in a sensuously souled world. "The air of winter is dense, hard, compressed. In the spring it has new vitality. It is light, mobile, and laden with a thousand palpitating odors from earth, grass, and sprouting leaves" (2009, p. 24). In this study, her work will be supplemented by the accounts of Anne Sullivan, Helen's teacher, and her biographer, John Macy, who lived with her for many years.

Keller's (2009) journals are filled with beautiful, subtle details of sense impressions, a reverence for the human imagination, and a child-like curiosity for the mysterious and hidden aspects of life. She writes:

> Other odors, instantaneous and fleeting, cause my
> heart to dilate joyously or contract with
> remembered grief. Even as I think of smells, my
> nose is full of scents that start awake sweet
> memories of summers gone and ripening grain
> fields far away. (p. 27)

In a way, Helen Keller will serve as a bridge between the olfactory research of the natural sciences and the theoretical perspectives of depth psychology. Through her writings it is possible to peer into a world seldom inhabited by the average person. She offers the reader an opportunity to somatically feel the significance and sensuousness of scents. With the exception of Hillman and Keller, the examples above illustrate the void, and thus the need, for a deep inquiry into the sense of smell from a depth psychological perspective. In order to accomplish this task, olfactory research from the natural sciences will be used to inform the existing literature of depth psychology.

Researcher's Relationship to the Topic and Autobiographical Origins

When I was 19 years old, my great uncle George passed away. My family inherited some of his belongings, among which were several boxes of books. As I sifted through the books, one caught my attention. It was a hardback copy of Leo Tolstoy's *War and Peace.* The copyright was 1956, which made it about 50 years old. I held the heavy book close to my face, flipped it open, and took several sniffs. It had an old, musty scent, like it had been resting untouched in a dusty den. I could also smell faint traces of the aroma of George's house, where I had visited occasionally. At once I began to see in my imagination my great uncle reading Tolstoy on his sofa or in his study. I wondered if he had bought the book new or as a used copy. What did the book smell like when George first bought it? Did anyone else ever hold this book and smell its musty pages, like I am now? What did the scent of the book mean to George, if anything?

It would be over a year before I embarked on reading Tolstoy's masterpiece, which spans over twelve hundred pages. I had just returned from traveling solo in Europe and was eager to explore the famous Russian novelist's dense work, this gift waiting for me, left by uncle George. For six months I sat in my soft, brown reading chair, devouring *War and Peace*, turning carefully its thin, off-white pages, full of English words I had yet to learn. Each flip of the page I breathed in its unique scent, vaguely aware of my ancestors who perhaps read Tolstoy, like my uncle George. There were times in the late evening when I pondered if George, in an unseen realm, was watching me hold and sniff his old, classic novel. I felt a tinge of excitement and a sense of pride knowing that by holding, reading, and smelling *War and Peace*, I was part of a lineage. Perhaps even Tolstoy himself was observing me.

The scent of that specific copy of *War and Peace* evoked images of Tolstoy himself writing in his large home estate; memories of my sister and me as children visiting uncle George, perusing *Mad Magazine*, watching football championships, drinking eggnog at Christmas. Yet if I were to get a different copy of *War and Peace*, it would not evoke the same images; for the multitude of

18

effects were in part due to the scent of that specific book and the unique associations to me at that time in my life.

I have developed a mostly unconscious behavior where whenever I pick up any book, especially if it is new to me, I open it and inhale several quick breaths. The smell of the book gives me a sense of its age and tone—its character so to speak. The ink, the paper used, and where the book has been, all contribute to its specific scent. Because the manufacturing and materials of paper and ink have evolved over time, their scents generally have a characteristic mark. I have smelled enough books in my life that I am now able to, in a few sniffs, roughly identify the decade that a particular book was printed.

I do not recall when I first started to smell books, certainly before I was nineteen, but my curiosity about scents goes back to early childhood. Perhaps it was observing my father frequently lift his collar and smell his shirt or watching him scrutinize the pasta my mother cooked to tell if it was boiled with tap or filtered water. I learned that scents could not only provide useful information but also add other sensory elements to any moment of experience. As a kid I explored and played in the alleys between the neighborhood streets. My friends and I would pluck honeysuckle flowers to smell and taste their sweet, liquid nectar from the base and stems. But even more enjoyable, jasmine flowers would explode in the alleys twice a year and we would collect large bundles to bring home. But at night my soul would get its richest experiences. I lived near the ocean and, often in the evening, the breeze would carry the aroma of wet sand, ocean salt, and mild fishiness to combine with the seductive night-blooming jasmine. The richness of experience was due to the complexity of all the elements combined: home, jasmine, happiness, the ocean, playing with friends, excitement, exploration, cool night air, and youthful innocence. Even at ten years old I sensed that whole experience was my "smellscape." Now in my mid-thirties, whenever I smell jasmine, especially if I am near the ocean, I re-enter that smellscape, moved by the scent and the images, and thus experience the full range of associations connected with those smells. My psyche truly understands what those scents mean.

The smell experiences from my early childhood to late teens have stayed with me to the present day. My current profession as a clinician of Chinese medicine has guided me to develop a close relationship with nature to prevent and treat illness. Not surprisingly, I became interested in using essential oils as an adjunct healing tool in my medical practice. After I studied extensively how to use essential oils therapeutically, I began to use them personally and clinically. Initially I used specific oils on acupuncture points, a method I learned several years ago from my herbalist teacher, Peter Holmes. I noticed that different people responded to the scents in unique ways. Some people were immediately repelled by common scents such as lavender and peppermint. Others reacted with notable emotions. For instance, I had an older woman smell a bottle of wintergreen mixed with blue tansy and within seconds she started to cry. When I asked her what triggered the emotions, she said the scent evoked a memory of her father, which took her back to childhood. She said it had been years since she had had such a vivid recollection of her past and was surprised by the strong effect that the oils elicited. Over time I have had similar essential oil experiences with my patients, as well as with friends and family. To observe the powerful effects that the aromas of essential oils have on some people has led me to question the forces at work that make up the whole experience. Therefore, my deep interest in scents is derived from both personal and professional experiences.

Statement of the Research Problem and Question

In contrast to the wide range of scientific research in vision and audition, olfaction has historically been given less attention. Nevertheless, olfactory research has not been completely neglected despite common claims of its absence. The sense of smell has been investigated in a variety of fields and disciplines, including chemistry, physics, and anthropology.

It is common knowledge that scents are closely tied to emotions and memory. Yet the idea that scent can be a psychic image is seldom discussed, even in the field of depth psychology, where a primary assumption is that psychic images have the function of making meaning. If, as Jung (1928/1969) proposed, the psyche is composed of images (p. 325), then an investigation of all the varied kinds of images—including scent images—is imperative to understanding the psyche. Perhaps the soul needs to attend to its own images in order to know itself, to affirm its own being. Alternatively, as Hillman says, "Maybe you're here not to understand anything but to appreciate what's here" (Shamdasani & Hillman, 2013, p. 172). In either case, not just any images will suffice; the soul needs images of depth, which resonate and echo, images that are meaningful. Because scent as image has not been directly examined for what it means for the human psyche, an effort to do so is the aim of my research.

In this dissertation, I will take a qualitative research approach and use the methodology of hermeneutics to interpret and synthesize relevant texts. A review of the literature in the natural sciences has revealed a wide range of olfactory topics. Subjects relevant to my research include emotion, memory, meaning, mental imagery, and attention to aromas. While it would appear that the natural sciences have already created a significant body of olfactory research, a depth psychological approach can contribute to the field by adding another perspective to olfactory experience.

A review of the literature in depth psychology has revealed a gap in the topic of scents and olfaction. What depth psychology does have, however, are a variety of profound scholars and a multitude of rich ideas that deal with the human soul. My research will therefore take the psyche as the starting place, and my aim will be to investigate the appearance and effects of scents within the human psyche. The depth psychological texts will intersect with research from the natural sciences so that each may inform one another. Specifically, my research presents an overview of the factors that give rise to meaningful scent images. I am hopeful that my research will bring attention to the importance of scents and the olfactory experience within the field of depth psychology.

My primary research question is as follows: if a function of psychic images is to create meaning, and if an aroma can qualify as a psychic image, how and when does a scent image become meaningful? In order to answer this, other auxiliary questions and related ideas must be examined. For instance, what are the elements or qualities that comprise scent as image? What is the essence of a meaningful scent image? How do we recognize or know an image has appeared? How does that process happen? In what ways are emotions and memory involved? What effect does reflection upon meaningful scent images have on the psyche? One hypothesis is that when strong emotions are associated with a particular smell and connected to a specific experience, together they form a psychic image, a "smellscape" that may later be reflected upon. "Smells, like images, are reflections," says Hillman (1979a, p. 140). How and when are smells reflections, and who exactly does the reflecting? It is toward the answers to these questions that my research will be driven.

Limitations and Delimitations of the Study

The methodology of this dissertation is qualitative research in hermeneutics, which has inherent limitations. I have intentionally set certain parameters—delimitations—so that the focus and scope of the research topic are specific and narrow enough to be thoroughly explored. Since hermeneutics is the interpretation and analysis of texts, I will not be using human subjects for this research to demonstrate empirical facts. Rather, text-based data will be used for dialectical or rhetorical arguments. Because my research will not be using quantitative methods, it will not show correlations, demonstrate probabilities, test empirically verifiable hypotheses, or make predictions. However, some generalizations will be made and certain conclusions put forth.

Given the limited scope of my research, many related ideas and topics will not be given due attention; what to keep or omit is a difficult decision. If I wish to highlight some feature of a text, then I must, as Gadamer (1975/2006) notes, "do so only by playing down or entirely suppressing other features" (p. 388). For instance, I will not investigate how scents might influence human behavior. Also, although scent-evoked memory involves experiences over time, I will not include developmental perspectives, such as how children and the elderly might experience scents differently.

Furthermore, I will make my base primarily within the domain of the personal psyche. Although depth psychology acknowledges the existence of a collective psyche, exploring that domain as well would require a complete research study in itself. In addition, although I will touch upon it briefly, I will only give limited attention to the discussion of dreams and scents—how and why individuals may or may not experience scents in their dreams, and what this might tell us about the human psyche. Despite the omission of the topics above, they are of great interest to me and I hope to include them in future research.

It would be easy to pretend that I can separate the researcher from the work itself, but this is not the case, as the researcher and the texts inform and influence each other. For "a person who is trying to understand a text is always projecting," writes Gadamer (1975/2006). "He projects a meaning for the text as a whole as soon as some initial meaning emerges in the text" (p. 269). I may not be able to avoid projecting meaning into the text, but at least I can be aware that I am doing so. Furthermore, in the same way that I cannot separate the researcher from the work, I cannot separate the method (hermeneutics) from the texts under investigation. As Palmer (1969) tersely states, "method and object cannot be separated: method has already delimited what we shall see" (p. 23). In the present case it is myself, using the method of hermeneutics, who will limit what I shall see, yet also make room for inevitable projections that can give rise to new meanings.

Gadamer (1975/2006) correctly narrows the focus: "The important thing is to be aware of one's own bias, so that the text can present itself in all its otherness and thus assert its own truth against one's own fore-meanings" (p. 272). My bias tends toward an interest in nature, poetry, playing, slowness in work, delicious food, craft beer and wines, sensual subtleties of the body, and preference of subjective over objective data. Furthermore, my profession in Chinese medicine has influenced how I think about and assimilate information, as well as what I attend to and what I tend to dismiss. Rather than linear and literal, my mind tends to function relationally, associatively, and metaphorically. Therefore, in order for the text to assert "its otherness" and "its own truth," I am required to take stock of my bias and preconceptions, or "fore-meanings." There seems to be no escaping the fact that all meaning and understanding inevitably involve some bias or prejudice.

Chapter 2

LITERATURE REVIEW

*The slightly tobaccoy odor of autumn
is perceptible in these pages.*
~Wallace Stevens, *Opus Posthumous*

*The image, in its simplicity,
has no need of scholarship.*
~Gaston Bachelard, *The Poetics of Space*

Through a review of the literature on olfaction, I will consider knowledge from the natural sciences, including biology, chemistry, and psychophysics; and a close reading of literature in depth psychology will be fundamental for placing the soul in a central position to be investigated. The next three chapters that comprise the thrust of my research will include a multitude of books and articles. However, the literature review below will limit the number of sources and therefore examine only primary and fundamental texts, those that are indispensable to my research questions.

Scientific Perspectives of Olfaction

Olfaction has traditionally concerned itself with perception and cognition in the fields of chemistry and biology. More recently these sciences have merged with neuroscience and psychology, comprising what olfactory pioneer-scientist, Trygg Engen (1991), called psychophysics, the interaction of physiology and psychological processes. The literature I will draw upon contains a variety of scientific studies on the nature of olfaction, but primarily I will be focused on psychophysical studies.

Cognitive neuroscientist and psychologist, Rachel Herz, is one of the world's experts on the psychology of smell. She has published over 70 original research papers and two popular books. Her most famous publication, *The Scent of Desire* (2007), is written for the average reader and is a thorough integration of olfactory research that touches on the physical, emotional, social, and sexual roles of scents. This book is valuable here for its broad olfactory topics and, in particular, the sections on emotion and memory.

Herz's recent scientific journal publications are useful for more detailed olfactory information. One such article, "The Role of Odor-Evoked Memory in Psychological and Physiological Health" (Herz, 2016), looks at how odors can evoke positive autobiographical memories, which ultimately improves health. Through a review of the literature she claims that, "Engaging in nostalgic reminiscence increases positive affect, bolsters self-esteem, strengthens the connection between one's past and present, produces feelings of social connectedness, elevates optimism, and infuses life with meaning" (p. 4). The content related to olfactory memory, emotion, and meaning is relevant and critical to my research.

A fascinating article that I will draw on is, "Attention to Odor Modulates Thalamocortical Connectivity in the Human Brain" (Plailly, Howard,

Gitelman, & Gottfried, 2008). The authors question the accepted view that our olfactory system functions without activation of the thalamus, which is a part of the brain that deals with sensory perception. Their results show that when we attend to an odor, a thalamic relay is required, if only to consciously analyze a smell (p. 5265). This study has important implications for the idea of attention that I will examine in my research.

Another article, published in the journal *Frontiers in Behavioral Neuroscience* (Saive, Royet, & Plailly, 2014), offers another perspective on scent-evoked memories. The authors review the neural bases of episodic (long-term) odor memory, highlighting the use of functional neuroimaging in olfactory research. What stands out in this article is its integrative approach to methodologies. Rather than exclusively using a laboratory-based inquiry or autobiographical approaches to studying olfaction, the researchers use a mixed-methods approach. "To investigate odor-evoked episodic memory, we recently developed an original laboratory-ecological approach" (p. 8). Their methodology takes into account many critical elements   that of context, history, emotion, and language. Their findings suggest that, "when an association between odors, spatial locations and contexts is encoded, the association forms an integrated representation retrievable by the participants" (p. 8). Thus, this article will serve in investigating the role of memory and meaningful scents.

"Scent-Evoked Nostalgia" (Reid, Green, Wildschut, & Sedikides, 2015) is an interesting article on the importance of nostalgia. Here the authors investigate the psychological implications of scent-induced nostalgia.

After conducting a series of studies, they found that, "Higher levels of scent-evoked nostalgia predicted higher levels of scent-evoked positive affect, self-esteem, self-continuity, optimism, social connectedness and meaning in life" (p. 162). This article highlights the connections between scent, memory, and meaning, important features for my research.

According to Herz (2007), a major question in the psychology of smell is: can we recall, that is, imagine fragrances? Herz concedes, "Though odors are exceptional triggers of memory, it is extremely difficult, if not impossible, to summon up the memory of an odor itself…can you truly capture the scent image of a peppermint in your mind's nose when the candy isn't there?" (pp. 85-86). Olfactory research has long failed to find evidence for olfactory imagery when the actual smell is not present. This is based on neuroimaging studies that show brain areas activated when a person imagines a visual object but not when imagining a scent (p. 86). Scent experts such as chefs and wine makers, who claim they can recall odors without the stimulus present, contradict such research findings. However, a more recent study (Royet, Delon-Martin, & Plailly, 2013) takes the opposite view. The authors claim that the existence of odor mental imagery in non-experts can be seen in the piriform cortex of the brain. The authors use "odor mental imagery" to mean odors that are mentally imagined, similar to imagining a visual scene or auditory sound. This study will therefore be useful to explore the implications of evoking an olfactory image without the physical scent present to activate the imagination.

This section of the literature review comprises the scientific perspectives of olfaction. The articles and books chosen represent the key subject areas of my research—namely olfactory sensation and perception, and olfaction's connection to memory, emotion, and imagery. These avenues of inquiry venture into the psychological nature of olfaction, but still remain in the paradigm of chemosensory studies. Yet an important finding in the scientific literature points to the personal and idiosyncratic nature of olfaction and thus will lead us in the direction of the depths of the human psyche—the topic of the next section in this literature review.

Depth Psychological Perspectives of Olfaction

The foundational author for this literature category is James Hillman. He is an advocate for the soul and all aspects of life pertaining to the psyche and has covered a wide range of psychological ideas over his career. Much of his thinking has a direct impact on this dissertation. In my view, Hillman's attention to the details and subtleties of human experience stands out among the depth psychological literature. To properly investigate the subtle sense of smell and the uniqueness of specific scents, it requires one to slow down enough to wrestle with or question ideas that often are overlooked or seemingly worn out. It takes a critical mind to pierce beyond the obvious appearance of forms and listen to what the soul has to say about what it has breathed in. Hillman reflects carefully, critically, and soulfully.

The first text by Hillman that gives voice to the soul's relationship to the senses is, *The Thought of the*

Heart and the Soul of the World (2014). This book considers the heart to be involved in all sense perceptions (rather than perception taking place only in the brain or mind). This is important because it grounds perception as "innately aesthetic" (p. 39), which may have implications for the engendering of meaningful scent images. "The world is a place of living images, and our hearts are the organs that tell us so" (p. 18). Furthermore, Hillman reminds us of the ancient connection of sensation and perception with the breath, which is, of course, a requirement to smelling anything. "The activity of perception or sensation in Greek is *aesthesis*, which means at root 'taking in' and 'breathing in'—a gasp, that primary aesthetic response" (pp. 39-40). Hillman's alternative perspective on sensation and perception will be valuable to enliven the experience of meaningful scent images.

Another important book, *Re-Visioning Psychology* (1975), is considered by many to be Hillman's most groundbreaking work. I will use it for its penetrating and thorough treatment of psychic images, and their intimate relationship to the human soul. He states, for instance, "Fantasy-images are both the raw materials and finished products of the psyche, and they are the privileged mode of access to knowledge of soul. Nothing is more primary" (p. xi).

Next, a series of articles by Hillman will be useful to explore several key ideas in this dissertation: meaning and scent as image. Spanning the time from 1977 to 1979, Hillman published "An Inquiry into Image" (1977), "Further Notes on Images" (1978), and "Image-Sense" (1979a). In these essays, connections are made between meaning and image. Following Jung, his starting point, or ontology, is "image is psyche." He emphasizes Jung's assertion that "image and meaning are identical," then amplifies this idea, "As shape emerges, meaning emerges. Image-making equals meaning" (1977, p. 75). Finally, nowhere are scents and the sense of smell given as much depth psychological attention as in "Image-Sense" (1979a). Here he makes a case that, "Odor, scent, and stench have no smell of their own, no content without a particular body. Smells cannot stand alone and must be linked to an image: rose-odor, toast-scent, refinery-stench" (p. 140). He also points out that, "A smell refers to a particular image in which the smell inheres. It conjures a unique event and favors discrimination among unique events" (p. 141). What I gain from these texts is that scent is placed within the context of psychic images. However, what is missing from these essays, is the subject of memory. For this topic, I must turn to a different book.

Tracking the White Rabbit: A Subversive View of Modern Culture (2002), written by Jungian Analyst Lyn Cowan, investigates the subject of memory with intelligence and insight. Her chapter titled, "False Memories, True Memory, and Maybes," takes a depth psychological perspective toward memory and psychic images. This chapter is best summarized by the following sentence: "The memory of an experience, the image of the emotions we experience, this is everything, for the image is where the soul resides" (p. 67). The important relationship the psyche may have with scent invariably involves memory. As noted above, the olfactory system is "very sensitive, learns quickly, and does not forget." For the evident reason that a scent can evoke an old memory with one unsuspecting inhale, the subject of memory must be investigated. Therefore, the work of Lyn Cowan will serve to take a depth psychological approach toward memory.

Helen Keller's (2009), *The World I Live in & Optimism: A Collection of Essays*, first published in 1903 when she was 23 years old, is an important text for my research. Though she was not a depth psychologist, Keller's writing is evocative, poetic, and embodied, that is, attuned to bodily sensations and imagistic impressions. Her short book contains essentially all the major ideas that I will be investigating. Her attention to the details of life that the sensate world provides, and her ability to poetically describe her experiences are relevant here. She draws the reader close: "Combine the endless space of air, the sun's warmth, the prevalence of fitful odors, the clouds that are described to my understanding spirit…and you will begin to feel surer of my mental landscape" (p. 43). Keller's personal writings will therefore complement the other depth psychological texts that are to be researched.

David Abram's, *The Spell of the Sensuous* (1996), offers rich material that bridges depth psychological aesthetics with a phenomenological perspective that is rooted in nature. The section in his book I am concerned with is called "The Forgetting and Remembering of the Air." Because scent molecules move through the air and inhalation is needed in order to smell, the subjects of wind, air, and breath will be included in my research. Abram writes that indigenous cultures have "a recognition of the air, the wind, and the breath, as aspects of a singularly sacred power. By virtue of its pervading presence, its utter invisibility, and its manifest influence…is the archetype of all that is ineffable, unknowable" (pp. 226-227). Faithful to the sensuous world, Abram emphasizes the reciprocity between the senses and the sensuous world. An example of the intimacy of aesthetics can be better understood by the following observation: "It is the air that most directly envelops us; the air, in other words, is that element that we are most intimately *in*" (p. 260).

Gaston Bachelard (1884-1962) is mostly known as a philosopher, but I also see him as a depth psychologist, for he places the dreaming soul and the poetic imagination at center stage. His books, *Air and Dreams* (1943/1988) and *The Poetics of Reverie* (1960/1969), will supplement my theoretical approach of scent as a psychic image. His work probes into the material imagination and differentiates formal images from dynamic images. "A psychology of the imagination that is concerned only with the structure of images ignores an essential and obvious characteristic that everyone recognizes: the *mobility of images*" (1943/1988, p. 2). This attunement toward the quality of images will help answer some of my research questions. Bachelard's writings also reveal the personal nature of scents: "Memories of odors from the past are recovered by closing our eyes…in the past as in the present, a beloved odor is the center of an intimacy" (1960/1969, p. 136). Thus, Bachelard's writings on the imagination will be a valuable resource for my research.

Organization of the Study

The following is a brief outline of the major topics and chapters of inquiry and will serve as the main body of research for this dissertation.

Chapter 3, Inner Smellscapes: Scent as Image, will trace olfaction from the first sensational inhale to the appearance and making of a psychic image. I will investigate the role of emotions, somatic sensations, and one's environment in the context of a specific scent.

Chapter 4, The Gasp: Memories of Beauty and Disgust, will examine the importance of memory as it relates to attractive and aversive aromas. What makes a scent pleasant and beautiful, or disgusting and ugly? I hypothesize that scent-evoked memories that constellate significant psychic images tend to be emotionally charged. More precisely, I will show how scents that evoke strong emotions are bound with the idea of aesthetics.

Chapter 5, Smell Your Reflections: The Mirrors of Meaning, will attempt to encapsulate the soul's reflective process on its experience of scent as a meaningful psychic image. I will make the case that paying attention to scents is important, especially those that evoke emotional memories, as they can engender meaning in the deepest corners of the human soul. Following the work of Hillman and Berry, two styles of reflection are proposed: zooming in and zooming out. The body's role in the reflective process and the self-knowledge derived from attending to somatic sensations is then discussed.

Chapter 6, Findings, reviews the psychological and clinical implications of my research. A concluding section to summarize my research findings will be followed by potential future directions this research may take.

Methodology

My research approach will be that of hermeneutics—the interpretation of texts. As the prominent philosopher Hans-Georg Gadamer (1975/2006) puts it, "Hermeneutics has traditionally understood itself as an art or technique" (p. 268). In other words, there is an art (rather than a science) to the interpretive technique of hermeneutics. Coppin and Nelson (2005) call the careful integration of texts, "the art of interpretive knowing" (p. 37). Interpretation itself is a kind of translation. In fact, hermeneutics finds the art of translation at its origin. "Hermeneutics in its early historical stages always involved linguistic translation, either as classical philosophical hermeneutics or as biblical hermeneutics. The phenomenon of translation is the very heart of hermeneutics" (Palmer, 1969, p. 31).

Therefore, it is my goal to "translate" the objective "hard facts" of natural science, and also give a poetic voice to the subjective experience of the individual. The integration of so-called objective knowledge with subjective experience should lead to a deeper understanding of both. While it is true that hermeneutics is concerned with understanding texts, Gadamer (1975/2006) reminds us:

> The translation of a text, however much the translator may have dwelt with and empathized with his author, cannot be simply a re-awakening of the original process in the writer's mind; rather, it is necessarily a re-creation of the text guided by

> the way the translator understands what it says. (p. 387)

In other words, during the process of textual interpretation, I must keep in mind that I am re-creating meaning that is based on my own understanding, and not merely summarizing or reproducing the author's ideas. As Gadamer emphasizes, "It is a hermeneutical necessity always to go beyond mere reconstruction" (p. 367). However, a hermeneutic methodology must place the material investigated into proper context. In Palmer's (1969) view:

> Meaning is something historical; it is a relationship of whole to parts seen by us from a given standpoint, at a given time, for a given combination of parts. It is not something above or outside history but a part of a hermeneutical circle always historically defined. Meaning and meaningfulness, then, are contextual; they are part of the situation. (p. 118)

This means to stay open to the interpretive "situation" and to allow the text to reveal itself in the moment. The research approach must be creative, flexible, and context dependent. As philosopher Paul Ricoeur (1981) writes, "no horizon is closed, since it is possible to place oneself in another point of view and in another culture" (p. 75). Ricoeur is saying that the researcher must stay aware of multiple perspectives while interpreting a text. This necessarily calls for "a faithful consideration of context and for a willingness to see knowledge gained through inquiry as always qualified by time, place, and representation" (Coppin & Nelson, 2005, p. 36). In other words, while conducting hermeneutical research the authors of the texts, as well as myself, need to be placed and understood in the context of when, where, and how the work appears.

My research places the soul as the central focus, which modern scientific research typically does not. "In perfecting only the rational tools of the ego, modernity has suffered from soul-less psychological research," notes Susan Rowland (2010, p. 162). If new perspectives are to be gained from this research, then a creative approach that takes old ideas and looks at them in new ways is beneficial. Hillman's approach through the lens of archetypal psychology will be important in this regard.

The archetypal approach, writes Moore (1989), is unique in that it is "rooted not in science but in aesthetics and imagination" (p. 15). Hillman's archetypal approach can therefore be seen as a "poetic basis of mind," where the manifestations of the psyche are experienced as fundamentally poetic, aesthetic, and metaphorical. "Archetypal," used here as an adjective, "seeks out the images in events that give rise to meaningfulness, value, and the full range of experience" (pp. 15-16).

A poetic or metaphorical relationship with the texts is needed to pierce through habitual and fixed ideas. Moreover, "a fundamental problem in hermeneutics," notes Palmer (1969), "is that of how an individual's horizon can be accommodated to that of the work" (p. 25). Consequently, I am not satisfied with narrow horizons or surface appearances of phenomena, and thus by "seeing through," trust that the deeper layers of a phenomenon will reveal themselves (Coppin & Nelson, 2005, p. 94). I understand the act of "seeing through" to mean one must not always take phenomena literally, but search out the metaphorical, poetic, or mythic interpretation. As philosopher Jean Grondin (1994) puts it, "Only in conversation, only in confrontation with another's thought that could also come to dwell within us, can we hope to get beyond the limits of our present horizon" (p. 124). The challenge, but also the potential reward, is to "find a new angle on experience and a new way of hearing old wisdom" (Moore, 1989, p. 2). Therefore, an archetypal approach that peers below surface phenomena is appropriate to my research and will serve fruitful.

Ethical Considerations

The theoretical and text-only nature of this research does not use human participants and, therefore, ethical concerns are minimal. I will, however, take great care to stay as close to the authors' original meaning as possible when I interpret their texts.

Chapter 3

INNER SMELLSCAPES: SCENT AS IMAGE

Orchil shakes out her long dark hair
That hides away the dying sun
And sheds faint odours through the air
~W.B. Yeats, *"The Madness of King Goll"*

You said, "Who did you come with?"
"The majestic imagination you gave me."
"Why did you come?"
"The musk of your wine was in the air."
~Rumi, *The Essential Rumi*

The first car that I bought not long after my sixteenth birthday was a 1987 Honda Accord. The man whom I bought the car from had apparently cleaned it well because, despite it being ten years old, the car retained a newish look and feel. Yet one of my first impressions I had was its particular smell, which certainly was not a brand new-car scent. It was a mix of car cleaner solution, dusty wool sheepskin seat covers, combined with perhaps the previous owner's own personal scent. The overall smell wasn't unpleasant, but I didn't care for it, mostly because it was "other"; it wasn't my scent. I recall having a strong urge to change the scent, that the car wasn't really mine until I made the smell more personal. The only immediate solution I could think of was to buy an air freshener.

So, before I showed my new car to anyone, or even before taking a cruise around town, I went to the closest gas station and bought a yellow, vanilla tree-shaped air freshener. They came two in a pack so I put one on my dashboard and the other in the back seat. It didn't take long before that sweet, artificial cardboard-vanilla scent filled my car. I felt excitement and pride, for not only buying my first car, but because I had already changed the smell, the car was already being transformed. About a week later, another smell left its indelible mark inside my car.

The first time I drove my own car to go surfing was a moment of great independence, happiness, and freedom. I had jittery sensations in my hands and feet and flutters in my belly. It was a hot day and I left my surfboard wax in the back seat of my car. When I returned from surfing the wax had completely melted. After I surveyed the wax damage on the seat I took a long and deep inhale. This particular surf wax smelled delicious (*Sex Wax* was the brand name), something like coconut, honey, and sea salt. I loved the way my new car smelled then, an amalgam of vanilla air freshener, surf wax, and the faint smell of the car before I bought it. As it turned out, that amalgam of fragrances became my car's identity—part of my identity as well—and would be the dominant scent for the three years that I owned it.

Sitting here now, twenty years later, I can easily bring to my imagination the scent of my first car. As I enter my inner smellscape, my soma feels giddy and energetic, as if I was sixteen again. During the first few weeks of owning my car I had feelings of nervous excitement combined with a sense of growing responsibility, independence, and heightened masculinity. Just like the incessant punk rock music from my car cassette deck that became the auditory backdrop to my teenage experiences, so too the scent of my Honda is like a vaporous thread that still connects hundreds of memories from decades ago.

My experience I just described, though personal and specific to myself, is not uncommon; most people during their life can recount one or several evocative and memorable experiences with smells. Yet I find it remarkable that out of millions of aromas we encounter in a lifetime so few stand out and leave such lasting impressions. Neuroscientist Rachel Herz (2016) notes: "The occurrence of personally meaningful odor-evoked memories is relatively rare" (p. 7). What accounts for those few striking scent experiences, those particular images that stay with us? This question leads into my research: how and when do scent images become meaningful? But before we can speak about meaningful images, it is necessary to investigate how and when a scent in general becomes an image.

Two Kinds of Images

Memories of the words of women,
All those things whereof
Man makes a superhuman
Mirror-resembling dream
~W.B. Yeats, "The Tower"

In Jung's view, according to Hillman (1975), images of the psyche are the fundamental facts of existence. "All consciousness depends on these images," elaborates Hillman. "Everything else—ideas of the mind, sensations of the body, perceptions of the world around us, beliefs, feelings, hungers—must present themselves as images in order to become experienced" (pp. 22-23). But, and this is a big but, not all images are the same. The purpose of this section is to differentiate two broad categories of images that are relevant to my research: perceptual images and memory images. This is a necessary move before I examine scent images specifically. Thus, when I write about scent images, we will be able to understand them as belonging to the categories of either perceptual or memory images, or both.

By "perceptual images," I mean those images that are formed almost instantly when our living soma is stimulated by sensory stimuli coming through any of our five senses. "Anything happening in the perceptual world can yield an image, can give rise to an image," says philosopher Edward Casey (as cited in Hillman, 2016d, p. 411). These images may be noticed by our perceiving ego, or quite frequently they are formed unconsciously. Jung (1923/1971) explains: "We know from experience, too, that sense perceptions which, either because of their slight intensity or because of the deflection of attention, do not reach conscious apperception, none the less become psychic contents through unconscious apperception" (p. 484). Whether formed consciously or unconsciously it seems as if perceptual images are imprints or replicas of sensory data. Our human capacity is thus situated in *physis*—our material nature and the body, which primarily refers to sensory perception "insofar as it replicates what is perceived" (Casey, 1974a, p. 25). Thus, one characteristic of perceptual images is the quick replication of what is perceived from the physical environment.

Perceptual images also appear to be involuntary. For instance, upon smelling a jug of milk and perceiving a sour odor, an image may automatically appear with an impression of "sourness" or "spoiled." These images may also be linked with other kinds of rotten food and drink images. Alternatively, we may willfully anticipate and imagine the negative effects if we were to drink the spoiled milk. I may perceive "sour milk," but the imaginative psyche appears to be co-creating the image along with sensory stimuli. The phenomena of linking or association is an important aspect in how the psyche functions. Jung (1909/1960) offers us a simple example describing the relationship between perceptual and memory images, which I will describe next:

> I meet an old friend in the street, and immediately there is formed in my brain an image, a functional unit: the image of my friend X. In this unit, or "molecule," we can distinguish three components, or "radicals": sense perception, intellectual components (ideas, memory images, judgments, etc.), and feeling tone. These three components are firmly united, so that if the memory image of X rises to the surface all the elements belonging to it usually come with it, too. (pp. 38-39)

In sum, perceptual images are imprints from our five senses and can be formed consciously or unconsciously. Further, perceptual images may arise involuntarily or by one's own volition. Finally, they are closely entwined with sensations, emotions, thoughts, and memory images, the last of which I now turn to.

By "memory images," I mean those images that we commonly think of when speaking or writing about memories from our past. They can occur directly or indirectly. Jung (1905/1970) explains direct memory:

> You have a direct memory when, for instance, you see a certain house and it then "comes into your mind" that a friend of yours lived there some years ago. You see the well-known house, and by the law of association the coexistent memory image of your friend enters your consciousness. (pp. 95-96)

In Jung's example the memory image (friend) is triggered by an environmental stimulus (house). Note that environmental stimuli can also be perceptual images and then become memory images. From my personal memory chest, I give another example of a direct memory image. When I smelled the stale beer on the floor, I was assaulted with numerous sad memories from my years in college. Direct memory can also occur by conscious imagining. For instance, I can still recall in all its details my bedroom from childhood. When I close my eyes, I can vividly see and hear the horrible car accident. In these examples I consciously evoke memory images without the presence of environmental stimuli.

An indirect memory image, however, is more complicated but nonetheless as important and possibly as common as direct memory images. Jung (1905/1970) elaborates:

> An indirect memory is different: I walk, deep in thought, past the house where my friend X used to live. I pay no attention either to the house or to the

street, but am thinking of some urgent business matter I have to attend to. Suddenly an unexpected image thrusts itself obtrusively between my thoughts: I see a scene in which X once discussed similar matters with me many years ago. I am surprised that this particular memory should come up, for the conversation was of no importance. Suddenly I realize that I am in the street where my friend once lived. In this case the association of the memory image with the house is indirect: I did not perceive the house consciously, for my thoughts distracted me from my surroundings too much. But the perception of the house nevertheless slipped into the dark background of consciousness and activated the association with X. As this association was too feebly accentuated to cross the threshold of consciousness, a common association had to intervene as an auxiliary. This mediating association is the memory image of the conversation that touched on matters similar to those now being revolved in my consciousness. In this way, the memory image of X enters the sphere of consciousness. (pp. 95-96)

The key elements I wish to point out here is that the indirect memory image was set within a particular context, mood, and scene (see Hillman, 1977). The image was unexpected ("suddenly…I see a scene"), and it carried a charge ("thrusts itself obtrusively between my thoughts").

At this point I would like to point out a quality that is characteristic of both direct and indirect memory: literal inaccuracy. This idea will be elaborated further in the next chapter on the memory of beauty and disgust, but I want to add a brief clarification within the context of memory images. If we think that our memories are like digital cameras that capture our experiences accurately, literally as they happened, we are mistaken. According to Lyn Cowan (2002), "what memory retains is the mood, the emotion, the subjective perception and experience of a reality—the psychic lens twisted a particular way—but not always the completely accurate reproduction of a literal event" (p. 58). In other words, memory is a phenomenon of "a" reality, not the only reality.

We can thus see how the psychic lens twisted in a particular way is what contributes to the making of the memory image, not just a literal memory "snapshot." From the perspective of Rachel Herz (2007), "Memory is more than just an accurate mental presentation of the past. In addition to the facts…memories have a personal, subjective, and emotional dimension" (p. 66). I would add that there is also a fantasy dimension to memory, an imaginative play that weaves its way through both perceptual and memory images. "Memory not only records," articulates Hillman (1975), "it also confabulates, that is, makes up imaginary happenings, wholly psychic events" (p. 18). The fantasy activity within our psyches adds, deletes, exaggerates, and condenses our experiences. Interestingly, our imagination may also be partially involved in the making of perceptual images. According to Casey (1974b), "It can be argued that no act of perceiving is wholly attenuated by non-perceptual elements, among which imaginative activity must be included" (p. 3). All of this psychic activity—environmental stimuli, memory, perceptions, sensations, imagination—appear to be necessary for the making of an image, whether a perceptual or memory image.

Having investigated two broad categories of images, I now turn to the specific process of making scent images.

The Making of Scent Images

*Man is primarily an imagemaker
and our psychic substance consists of images;
our being is imaginal being,
an existence in imagination.
We are indeed such stuff
as dreams are made on.*
~James Hillman, *Re-Visioning Psychology*

*The fairest thing in nature, a flower,
still has its roots in earth and manure;
and in the perfume there hovers still the faint
strange scent of earth, the under-earth in all its
heavy humidity and darkness.*
~D.H. Lawrence, *Introduction to Pansies*

I wish to begin my inquiry into the making of scent images with Jung (1933/1969a), who wrote: "My sense impressions…are psychic images, and these alone constitute my immediate objects of my consciousness" (p. 353). Elsewhere Jung explains that, "what happens in the spinal cord is transmitted to the perceiving ego in the form of a record, or image, which one can furnish with names and concepts" (1928/1969, p. 322). I take these two passages to mean that we first have a (scent) sensation, and then an image appears, followed by (potentially) names and concepts—i.e. perception. But is this accurate? Have I fallen into the trap of materialism that Hillman (1975) warns against, which "regards the way things are in the perceptual world of things, facts and sense-realities to be the primary mode?" (p. 84). For materialism "insists that material reality is first and psychic reality must conform with it: *psyche* must obey the laws of *physis* and imagination follow perception" (p. 84). I wish to return to Jung's conception of the relationship between the spinal cord, the ego, image, and concepts. I must point out that it is possible for the sequence of events to vary, that is, sensations, images, and perceptions could occur simultaneously, or the order even reversed. For instance, I may conceptualize the idea of love and then fantasize what my "dream girl" would smell like, which is then followed by beautiful images of her, coinciding with somatic sensations of warmth and lightness. In any case, the main point I want to make here is that I believe Jung is writing about the making of perceptual images, in contrast to memory images, as I have outlined above.

A perceptual image in Jung's sense can be understood as an intermediary between environmental stimuli and the ego, "a third possibility between mind and world," elaborates Hillman (2014, p. 11). Interestingly, Aristotle and Kant, according to Casey (1974b), viewed the imagination as an "intermediary between sensation and thought. 'The soul never thinks without an image,' said Aristotle, and Kant echoes this by calling the image a 'mediating representation'" (p. 5). In the same manner, scholar Henry Corbin (1972) offers this perspective: "The word *imago* can give us the term *imaginal* in addition to the regular derivative *imaginary*. We would thus have the imaginal world as an intermediary between the sensible world and the intelligible world" (p. 15). Further, Casey writes of this imaginal world as a "self-presenting domain of apparitional figures," and "teeming with transmuted substances, subtilized sensuous forms, and legions of figures each with a proper place within the endlessly variegated topography" (1974a, pp. 25-27). In other words, perceptual images or figures appear to be situated in a self-presenting imaginal world that is neither exclusively internal nor external.

For some, this "imaginal world" may seem magical, fanciful, or unreal. But perhaps, as Casey (1974a) professes, "it is a magical act in the spirit of what Paracelsus called 'true imagination,' which transmutes gross matter into subtle, immaterial bodies" (p. 22). Thus, we have "true imagination"—images, not physically real, but psychically real as "subtle bodies." It would seem, then, that Jung, Hillman, Aristotle, Kant, Corbin, and Casey are pointing toward the same ontology, the making or appearance of psychic images as a reality of the psyche.

At this point an analogy may be helpful to understand the imagination's role in the making of scent images. Helen Keller (2009) describes a house that is unfamiliar to her, which at first has

> no general effect or harmony of detail. It is not a complete conception, but a collection of object-impressions that, as they come to me, are disconnected and isolated. But my mind is full of associations, sensations, theories, and with them it constructs the house...the silent worker is

imagination which decrees reality out of chaos. (p. 4)

I chose Keller's experience of her imagination constructing a house that she could not see or hear as an analogy for how we may conceive of making scent images. It is as if our psyches collect and gather all available data to build rich images such as a builder gathers materials to construct a house. However, Casey (1974b) points out that, "In imagining we are not restricted to imagining disparate and unrelated objects or events. We can also entertain whole complexes of simultaneously apprehended entities" (p. 8). In other words, our psyche can differentiate specific sensory impressions to make images, or it can synthesize various impressions into one complex whole image, as Keller does with the house. So, whereas images can be seen as nouns—sense impressions or objects of perception, imagination—the "silent worker"—acts as a dynamic verb, making and creating images.

But when it comes to odors as sense impressions, we must contend with two formidable facts about olfaction. First, "scent molecules exist in the air, but we can only register some of them as 'smells,'" notes sensory psychologist, Avery Gilbert (2008, p. 25). In order for aromas to be perceived, scent molecules must be "light enough to evaporate and be carried on air currents to our nose." If the molecules do make it to our nose, "the sensory cells in our nose convert a chemical signal (the molecule) into an electrical signal (a nerve impulse) that travels up the olfactory nerves to the brain for interpretation" (pp. 25-26). Thus, if scents are too heavy and cannot evaporate, if air currents are minimal, or the nose and brain function poorly, many scents in the environment never make it to the brain for interpretation.

Second, in the course of a day the average person smells a multitude of scents, yet most fragrances will never reach conscious awareness. "For the most part, odor perception functions without conscious awareness while monitoring the chemical environment" (Engen, 1991, p. xii). So, what about those sense impressions that do not cross the threshold of consciousness and do not therefore present themselves as "objects of consciousness"? Can we still consider them psychic images? Again, we turn to Jung (1954/1969):

> The idea of a threshold presupposes a mode of observation in terms of energy, according to which consciousness of psychic contents is essentially dependent upon their intensity, that is, their energy. Just as only a stimulus of certain intensity is powerful enough to cross the threshold, so it may with some justice be assumed that other psychic contents too must possess a higher energy-potential if they are to get across. If they possess only a small amount of energy they remain subliminal, like the corresponding sense perceptions. (p. 172)

From Jung's statement we can conclude that if sensory stimuli do not have enough energy or evocative power to become objects of consciousness, we cannot therefore consider them psychic images. Thus, when it comes to sense impressions from odors we can say that not all odorants that reach the brain become scent images. So, the first quality or condition that is needed for the making of a scent image is the strength of its energetic charge—its ability to evoke. However, this cannot be the only condition, so what are the other factors that engender an odorant to become a scent image? In other words, what else differentiates a scent image from a non-scent image?

But before I investigate this topic further, I must point out that scent images can be made from one specific odor, like the aroma of gasoline, for instance, or from a combination of several odors, like my great-grandmother's house that reeked of musty violets, apples, and rice cakes. In the perfume industry a combination of odors is called *accords*, which are "mixtures of raw materials that go together particularly well…individual ingredients recede and whole fragrances emerge" (Gilbert, 2008, p. 12). Truer to our experience, however, scent combinations are typically linked in disharmonious, idiosyncratic fashion rather than in nice synthetic accords.

I will offer another personal example. For several years during my childhood my uncle Darrell lived in a small trailer in the alley behind my house. He would use the bathroom and kitchen inside our house, but otherwise the trailer was his home and to my knowledge nobody ever went inside. But one night when I was about eight years old he let me spend the night in the trailer with him. As soon as I walked inside it was as if I entered into a different culture and time in history. The old tin trailer had a musty, damp, metallic, chilly, slightly moldy smell, mixed with the scent of old biblical books, a down sleeping bag, fresh grass, and salty soil. It smelled dirty yet I knew it wasn't; Uncle kept it clean and tidy, like a priest. I liked it because it smelled utterly like nothing I had inhaled before.

Before sleeping that night, I had eaten hot dogs and popcorn for dinner. After a few hours of sleeping I awoke feeling sick and I vomited on the trailer floor. I felt ashamed but Uncle didn't make me feel bad about it. Despite spending the night sick, I recall that I still enjoyed sleeping in such an unusual place. In the years that followed I would occasionally enter Uncle's trailer and it always smelled the same, but with the added memory of hotdog and popcorn vomit that could never completely vanish from my memory. Many would doubt that at this moment I could actually recall that strange mix of scents from my uncle's trailer almost thirty years ago; but, alas, the image is still here.

This story illustrates the peculiar and discordant odor combinations that we often experience in our lives. I wish to point out that not only were the aromas particular to my experience, but that they stuck with me; the scent images adhered within my psyche and left a lasting impression. This quality of adherence—that images stick—will be developed later in this chapter. So, we have odor combinations that are typically idiosyncratic and that also stick with us. However, when I first asked people during my fieldwork project about pleasant and unpleasant scents, I frequently received generic responses such as "I like the smell of pizza and beer," or "my wife's perfume is nice." But after spending more time talking in depth about scent preferences and experiences, most people revealed multiple scent associations and odor memories that were quite specific and idiosyncratic. One woman once told me about her first job, which was in an office at a dairy plant. In the summer there was a stench of spoiled milk, combined with diesel fuel and "office scents," like carpet, wood, and paper. "The result of such a blending is sometimes a discordant trying of strings far removed from a melody, very far from a symphony," imparts Helen Keller (2009, p. 41).

But perhaps Nature has her own kind of scent symphonies? Gilbert (2008) offers a poetic image to this idea: "Most aromas in nature are elaborate bouquets, mixtures of dozens if not hundreds of different molecules" (p. 26). Sometimes we experience one simple odor and that is all that's needed for the beginning of a scent image. On other occasions we inhale an evocative and complex "bouquet." For us human "imagemakers," both single and complex aromas each have their role in the engendering of scent images.

Let us return to the question of what distinguishes a scent image from a non-scent image. So far, I have been outlining the foundations for the making of scent images. We have proposed that environmental stimuli or sense impressions become psychic contents either consciously or unconsciously. At this point these psychic contents are not yet necessarily images. We have found that consciousness of psychic contents is essentially dependent upon their intensity, whether the psychic contents have a strong enough energic charge to cross an assumed threshold. If the psychic contents do possess sufficient intensity, they may become perceptual or memory images. These images may not be objectively or physically real but are considered to be subjectively or psychically real.

Further, we have observed that this subjectivity, or ego, is in close relationship with the imagination, an intermediate imaginal realm where fantasy activity colors and textures all psychic experiences. Finally, when it comes to scent images, we have identified four essential qualities that appear to be necessary for the formation of the scent image. These qualities—evocative, idiosyncratic, emotionally-somatically based, and stickiness of the image—will now be examined in greater detail.

The Evocation of the Image

Why, there are moments when the scent is so
powerful that I almost faint
with delight in inhaling it!
~Emile Zola, *Three Cities*

She is alone
With all the old nocturnal smells
That cross and cross across her brain
~T.S. Eliot, *"Rhapsody on a Windy Night"*

Hillman (2016d) asks two important questions: "How does an image appear before we try to define it? What is the experiential moment of an appearance of an image?" (p. 420). In other words, what is the phenomenology of an image? What is the lived experience of an image before names, definitions, and concepts take hold? When it comes to scent images this is not always easy to accomplish, as the source of the odor is known almost immediately as perception occurs in our brain. For instance, a common scent like pizza will appear to us almost simultaneously with the label "pizza," as well as somatic sensations, emotions, and associative images. The definition of an odorant is given with the sensation and image. However, with some odors we may not know the source right away, if ever. When the scent is strong enough we may be compelled to search out its source. It is like catching a whiff of your neighbor's dinner though an open window and sniffing a few times before labeling the source of the smell. In between the sniffs and the pinning down of the odor source, you might notice your belly rumble and a childish joy rise up your spine, but not yet knowing why. The image has arrived or is in the process of arriving. Then…aha! The neighbors are cooking pasta—marinara sauce with lots of basil, just like Mom used to make. Whoosh! A flood of images from childhood present themselves as you continue to sniff your neighbor's dinner.

Casey says, "dreams carry images, words carry images, paintings carry images—but differently" (as cited in Hillman, 2016d, p. 425). To this I would add: scents carry images. But how do we recognize or know a scent image has arrived?

As we determined above, for a scent image to be noticed by the ego it must contain a strong enough energetic or emotional charge. The image must have a kind of edge or intensity to it. Casey says it like this: "The image insists—demands to be seen, insists on being seen. That has a lot to do with the special intensity or poignancy…something has to have a certain, as it were, edge to reach your perception" (as cited in Hillman, 2016d, pp. 423-424). I wish to point out that Casey uses the verb "to see" when referring to the demands of images. But let me clarify that when Hillman, Casey, and other depth psychologists use the word image, they are not writing solely about an optical experience, something that refers only to vision and sight. Hillman (1999) makes an important distinction:

> Because consciousness has become identified with the sense of sight…images have been conceived as visual representations, rather than as presentations of significance, or even as presences. As we feel feelings, sense sensations, think thoughts, so we imagine images. We do not have to see them *literally*. We do not literally see the images in poems or the characters in novels, or even those in paintings. We "see" images with imagination. (p. 183)

Another way of saying that images "insist on being seen" is to say that images want their presence known, felt, or acknowledged. How do we know this? We know this because the images are simply there; they present themselves, and often against our will. As Hillman writes, images present themselves as a kind of display, as if they are living beings with a presence. It is like walking outside and seeing a full moon and unable to look away. The moon commands her presence: "Hey, over here, look at me, pay attention to me, I am here." Or it is like a vague mood we find ourselves in and no matter how we try to dismiss the mood it remains until we feel into it, or at least acknowledge that it exists. It is as if the image has a charge or life force of its own.

But how do we know if an image carries a charge? One way we can tell, according to Hillman (1978), is that "images evoke" (p. 168). Images can evoke feelings, ideas, memories, insights, somatic sensations, as well as constellate other images. Let me share an experience I had recently. While out shopping one afternoon I walked past a supermarket and was struck by a strong aroma of fried chicken. Apparently, the supermarket was advertising by strategically placing fried chicken near the entrance. It was a warm day and the smell seemed especially strong as if there were fans blowing the food odor into the parking lot. For me the scent was quite disgusting. Oily, fatty, unhealthy meat for a mostly vegetarian person such as myself is disturbing. Fortunately, I did not have to inhale it for too long, but my body was already aroused—nausea, headache, and a feeling of anger in my jaw along with images of the corporate distribution of poor quality meat, and sadness in my chest coupled with images of consumers who buy and eat such food. I could not help but see images of the chickens themselves—raised in terrible conditions, killed for profit, driven hundreds of miles to be heated and sold at my local supermarket. The fried chicken scent evoked a flurry of unpleasant images that pushed me a little off balance for some time afterward.

So, how do we explain such evocative images? Sensory physiology has determined that the human body is governed by a sensorimotor system. "The sensory motor system functions as a 'closed-loop feedback system' within the soma. We cannot sense without acting, and we cannot act without sensing," notes Thomas Hanna (1995, p. 345). Thus, a charged image (if understood as a sense perception) will always evoke a motor response within us. This response could vary from a subtle sigh, a smile, or tightening of our calf muscles, to more pronounced reactions such as crying, running away, or vomiting. Further, sensations will invariably involve emotions as well. "Whatever the theoretical point of view adopted…emotions are viewed as intelligent interfaces that mediate environmental input to adaptive output" (Delplanque et al., 2012, p. 894). Based on the sensorimotor system, therefore, some kind of physical and emotional change or adaptation will occur; we have been evoked somatically and psychically.

For example, "many sorts of images," explains Hillman (1999), "written, painted, modeled in clay, projected on the television glass, evoke a voyeuristic response. We find it hard to turn away because we are subliminally turned on. Images arouse" (p. 110). Not only do images turn us on and draw us in by their evocative and arousing powers, they can also send us fleeing.

We cannot only speak about pleasant images, but we must necessarily include the ugly, disgusting, and unpleasant ones as well. These too evoke and arouse, though differently. In the case of scent images, we may feel intense disgust, anger, or sadness embedded within a particular aroma. For instance, upon smelling Jose Quervo tequila my stomach used to cramp and a headache ensued, followed by shameful images of myself lying sick on a bathroom floor. For many years I was "assaulted" by the scent of Mr. Quervo, both emotionally and somatically. Hillman (1975) writes about the "exceptionally moving power" of pathologized images, those of sickness, disgust, and disease: "We start up, afflicted, haunted through the day, psychologically on edge. The pathologized images have moved the soul in several ways: we are afraid; we feel vulnerable and in danger…a sickened image vitally afflicts us" (p. 83). Here with pathologized images we again see the quality of intensity, an edge and emotional charge of the image that tells of its arrival. Whether pleasant or unpleasant, the image has an ability to move us, provoke us psychically as well as somatically.

Sometimes the pleasant and unpleasant are woven together and move us at the same instant. This is more difficult to describe in words and seems to go against the typical dualistic notions of hedonic scent responses. The accomplished perfumer, Sophia Grojsman, understands this experience: "When I first saw Picasso's *Guernica*, it was disturbing. I was horrified and fascinated at the same time. It was disturbing, but also deeply moving. Perfumes do that, too—shock and fascinate us. They disturb us" (as cited in Ackerman, 1990, p. 51). A scent that is vague, boring, or inconsequential will not be felt with much energetic charge, and thus will not form an image within the psyche.

Let me push this idea a little further and ask how do we know what amount of charge is enough to make an image? Is it possible to measure or quantify this energetic charge? Jung's (1954/1969) view is that, "In psychology the exact measurement of quantities is replaced by an approximate determination of intensities, for which purpose, in strictest contrast to physics, we enlist the function of *feeling* (valuation)" (pp. 233-234). Thus, according to Jung, there is no way to quantifiably determine the intensity or energetic charge of an image. Of course, science has come a long way since Jung's time, and it is possible that instrumentation has been developed which can now measure image intensity, but I have yet to read any recent studies that dispute Jung's claim. Perhaps we are in the realm of the immeasurable "subtle body," as thinkers such as Casey, Paracelsus, and Jung have described. Jungian analyst Marion Woodman (1984) writes, "It is the energy of the images that constitute what Jung, drawing upon an ancient tradition, called 'the subtle body'" (p. 31). In this sense the "energy of the image" would correspond to the emotional intensity that is bound with the image. So how much energetic charge is needed to make an image is different for each person and is bound by perceived feeling intensity. It thus appears that we are left with our subjective feelings, the emotions pulsing through our soma as our trustworthy guides.

Arousal, stimulation, provocation, and agitation—all are ways by which images show us their arrival. When speaking of evocation, we are necessarily speaking about emotions and the human soma, the experience of feelings within our own body. We may experience a change in our heartbeat, a fluctuation of body temperature, an expansion or constriction in a certain area of our body, or a rumbling in our stomachs. Trygg Engen (1982) makes an important observation:

> Those who write about perception have a general tendency to think in terms of cognition. This may not be the best approach for the perception of odor, if odor is to emotion what vision is to cognition. When odor is involved it may well cause a feeling before it elicits a concern with the meaning of the odor. (p. 155)

What Engen is stressing here is the importance of emotions and feelings in odor perception. Rodaway (1994) would agree with Engen: "Smells are not neatly defined objects in the sense of visual objects but experiences of intensities, more like those of pain and joy" (p. 65). Thus, we can see emotion as being a necessary quality for the evocation that contributes to the making of a scent image.

We therefore need to investigate the somatic experience of emotion in the context of olfaction.

The Emotional and Embodied Image

Emotion is the moment when steel meets flint
and a spark is struck forth,
for emotion is the chief source of consciousness.
~C.G. Jung, *Psychological Aspects*
of the Mother Archetype

The imagination dominates emotional life.
~Gaston Bachelard, *Air and Dreams*

Feelings stir as images move.
~James Hillman, *The Thought of the Heart*

We have started with the investigation of the making of scent images by looking at the ways in which we know an image has arrived in our awareness. The first characteristic we determined is that the image has an energetic charge that evokes or arouses us in some way. In other words, the scent image carries enough intensity or has an edge to it so that it crosses the threshold of consciousness and induces an affect, an emotional response that is felt somatically. The purpose of this section therefore is to unfold the role of emotions and feelings in the body as they relate to scent images.

To speak or write about emotions is tricky in part because the operational definition of emotion itself is variable and dependent upon who establishes it. For instance, psychologist Paul Ekman (2003) takes a Darwinian approach, and has proposed that all humans have six primary or basic emotions—joy, sadness, anger, fear, disgust, and surprise—which universally show up in our facial expressions. But, as Ekman points out, we also have secondary emotions, many of which are more complex, such as shame, jealously, and envy (pp. xx-xxi). When it comes to describing scent-evoked emotions, we typically resort to oversimplifications and dualisms such as "good smell, bad smell." Even scientific literature tends to limit itself when describing either "pleasant or unpleasant odors." For instance, one article published in the *Journal of Clinical and Experimental Neuropsychology* is titled "Associations to Smell are More Pleasant Than to Sound" (Mohr, Rohrenbach, Landis, & Regard, 2001).

However, in spite of the complexities about the categorical nature of emotions, "there is an agreement that emotions contain subjective feelings, action tendencies, physiological arousal, cognitive processes, and expressive motor behavior" (Delplanque et al., 2012, p. 894). These scientists are acknowledging that emotions are a primary reality of our human experience, and perhaps due to their complexity, defy strict categorical labels and definitions. Published in the journal *Cognition and Emotion*, these same researchers counter Ekman's basic emotion theory: "By focusing on a small number of evolutionarily based basic emotions, one downplays the more complex forms of emotional processes, especially affective feeling states produced by odours that do not directly serve adaptive behavioral functions linked to olfaction, such as nostalgia" (p. 893). In other words, emotions and feeling states are complex and to reduce them to a few basic ones is to limit the scope of human experience.

We are thus confronted with a common problem of semantics, that is, the limitations of language itself, which frequently do not adequately express our direct scent experiences. "Because of the specificity of the emotional effects of odours, the terms derived from traditional models of emotion are unlikely to optimally account for odour-associated feelings" (Delplanque et al., 2012, p. 885). There are two problems here that I wish to point out. First, we have difficult describing our emotions. The second are the limitations due to traditional models of odor characterizations. This subject of language will be further developed in the next chapter. But what I want to stress here is that it is imperative to be specific and particular when describing our scent evoked emotions, rather than resort to established models of emotional categories. "What a miracle it is," writes Hillman (1975), "to find the right words, words that carry soul accurately, where thought, image, and feeling interweave" (p. 217).

To find the right words for describing emotions is a difficult task indeed. Herz (2007) elucidates this problem: "The experiences of emotion and olfaction are similarly primal, visceral, and removed from verbal-semantic analysis. We have the same kind of difficulty using words to deconstruct our emotional experiences as we have articulating our experiences of smell" (p. 16). Perhaps instead of using oversimplified words like good/bad, pleasant/unpleasant, it is more effective to speak metaphorically, poetically, imagistically, or use somatic descriptions. For, as Hillman (1978) points out, "the image speaks just as the world speaks, concretely, and as dreams speak, sensately. Images bring body and concepts remove body" (p. 169).

For example, when I smell night-blooming jasmine, I sometimes feel as if a woman is flirting with me by brushing her fingers across my neck and chest. My chest will sometimes expand and my eyes open wide as I inhale. Sometimes I even hear Jasmine whisper seductively to me, "Hello there...." Does this not convey more than if I were to say, "Wow, this jasmine smells so good"? "Metaphors and word-pictures take us deeper into psyche," imparts Lyn Cowan (2002), "where image is the language of the soul" (p. 33).

In the context of my research I am less concerned with names, concepts, and categories of emotions. Regarding scent images, what is more important here is that we are moved emotionally—physiologically, somatically—that we have been altered or affected in some way. "Often we don't experience the reality of a psychic image until we feel it in our body," imparts Marion Woodman (1993, p. 118). Feelings can occur somatically through, for example, changes in our blood pressure or breathing, relaxing or tightening of our muscles, or a fluctuation in body temperature. The alteration can also occur through affect. Jung (1923/1971) often uses "emotion" and "affect" synonymously. In his own words: "I regard affect on the one hand as a psychic feeling-state and on the other as a physiological innervation-state, each of which has a cumulative, reciprocal effect on the other" (pp. 411-412). To clarify further Jung gives us a simple example:

> The fire I see arouses emotional reactions of a
> pleasant or unpleasant nature, and the memory
> images thus stimulated bring with them
> concomitant emotional phenomena which are

> known as *feeling tones*. In this way an object
> appears to us as pleasant, desirable, and beautiful,
> or as unpleasant, disgusting, ugly, and so on. In
> ordinary speech this process is called *feeling*.
> (1931/1969, p. 141)

Jung's definition of affect and his fire example highlight
and reveal the essential qualities of somatics—that is, the
experience of the body from within, which is a feeling
tone that is both psychic and bodily. Thus, we can see that
emotions are complex, involving both the psyche and
soma. It is for this reason that I will make use of Eugene
Gendlin's (1978) idea of the "felt sense":

> A felt sense is not an emotion like anger, fear, hate,
> joy, or anxiety. It is a sense of your *total* emotional
> situation, a feel of many things together, in which
> an emotion can be embedded or from which an
> emotion is produced. (p. 97)

The total emotional situation is, I believe, closer to our
lived experience, which is usually a web of complex
emotions, thoughts, images, moods, and somatic
sensations. Instead of trying to label and extract one word
for an emotion, the idea of the felt sense is able to
encompass our emotional experiences in a simple way
without being reductive.

But what happens if we are not in tune with our
body, if we are dissociated or numb to our bodily feelings?
Will we then be deprived of experiencing a scent image
fully? To be disconnected from our somatic feelings and
deprived of rich images would be a significant loss,
because "emotional life is really hungry for images,"
affirms Bachelard (1943/1988, p. 115).

A passage from D. H. Lawrence (1959) stresses the importance of emotions felt in our body:

> The body's life is the life of sensations and emotions. The body feels real hunger, real thirst, real joy in the sun or the snow, real pleasure in the smell of roses or the look of a lilac bush; real anger, real sorrow, real love, real tenderness, real warmth, real passion, real hate, real grief. All the emotions belong to the body, and are only recognized by the mind. We may hear the most sorrowful piece of news, and only feel a mental excitement. Then, hours after, perhaps in sleep, the awareness may reach the bodily centres, and true grief wrings the heart. (p. 88)

Lawrence is making a strong case for just how central and immediate our bodies are to all facets of our life. His emphasis on the body is perhaps necessary to underscore how essential and intimate our emotional and somatic being is to our lived experience as humans. When it comes to olfactory sensations and emotions, however, the feelings are usually immediate, rather than hours later, like Lawrence observes. Nevertheless, olfactory research supports the significant connection scents have with emotions. "The neurological interconnection between the sense of smell (olfaction) and emotion is uniquely intimate. The areas of the brain that process smell and emotion are as intertwined and codependent as any two regions in the brain could possibly be" (Herz, 2007, p. 3). It is therefore the intelligent, emotional soma that provides vital information of a felt sense to our ego that a scent image may be present.

Now, let us return to the task at hand. When we want to inquire if a sense impression "evokes," we can ask ourselves: Do I feel touched or untouched? Or we can follow Bachelard (1943/1988), who suggests we ask ourselves to what extent we feel lighter or heavier (p. 10). I can also ask if there is a felt sense in my body that indicates I have been moved, aroused, or provoked by something or someone? "Only very special words or images make a body shift in the felt sense. When that happens, the body has changed, learned, spoken more clearly, moved forward, lived further" (Gendlin, 1978, p. 166). For instance, one of my patients upon smelling lime essential oil was instantly triggered by strong feelings and images from his childhood where he worked in his father's citrus orchard. He leaned forward in his chair, smiled, and quickened his voice as he recounted to me his life long ago in the citrus orchards. He said the lime oil encapsulated ten years of happiness that no other scent could. This example demonstrates a common feature of scent images, that is, "when an aroma triggers recall, you are caught in a wave of emotion and evocation like no other" (Herz, 2007, p. 74). Not all scents will bring forth an image or a strong emotional reaction of course, but Herz is implying that when it does happen it is powerful and therefore obvious to the ego; we know when we have been touched—we feel it in our pulsing soma.

Yet despite the fact that my patient was aroused by lime essential oil, his image of the citrus orchard was unique; no other person would have the exact same image arrive into his or her awareness. Likewise, we know that jasmine is a popular fragrance worldwide, yet we would be surprised to find one other person on the planet (besides me) who upon smelling the white blossoms has images of a woman who flirts and whispers seductively. The observation that scent images are unique and particular leads us to the next section.

The Idiosyncratic Image

The individual is not the sum of his common
impressions but of his unusual ones.
~Gaston Bachelard, *Water and Dreams*

In real life there is no such person
as the average man.
There are only particular men, women
and children, each with his or her inborn
idiosyncrasies of mind and body.
~Aldous Huxley, *Brave New World Revisited*

In Great Eternity every particular form
gives forth or emanates
Its own peculiar light, and the form
is the Divine Vision
~William Blake, *"Brotherhood and Restriction"*

So far, we have determined that scent images are evocative, emotional, and embodied. But do we all respond to the same scent images in the same way? The answer is no, according to Trygg Engen (1982), who proposes that "idiosyncratic responses are typical for odors; for example, 'smell of a dusty old book in the John Hay library'…it seems fitting to describe odor language as both idiosyncratic and impoverished" (p. 103-106). If

Engen is correct, what accounts for these idiosyncratic odor responses (somatic and verbal) and how does the peculiar nature of olfactory responses contribute to the making of a scent image?

If we were to ask people about their personal and specific scent experiences we would invariably hear emotional and feeling descriptions of some kind. Like I explored in the previous section, we are here again describing the felt sense, as it were. "The associations that occur between emotions and odors are based on our personal experiences," notes Herz (2007), "and may not be predictable; thus, the pleasure or pain that odors elicit is not the same for all of us" (p. 114). Along a similar thought line, Rodaway (1994) observes that the olfactory sense "is strongly associated with the emotions and the encounter with specific smells and smell intensities excite particular emotional responses—though such correlations are not always simple nor can be generalized for all individuals or cultures" (pp. 64-65). If our emotional scent experiences are complicated, unique, and cannot be generalized, then we are compelled to seek out the particulars.

So, what makes a scent experience stand out? In Jung's (1931/1969) view: "When I characterize something as 'peculiar,' I am referring to the special feeling tone which that thing has. The feeling tone implies an evaluation" (p. 141). The "special feeling tone" must then be subjectively oriented toward a first-person perspective that stands out from ordinary experiences. "By localizing the feeling," writes Patricia Berry (2008), "one gains a kind of precision within a particular image and context. The psychic imagination (as does the poetic) proceeds by means of differentiation" (p. 115). Therefore, a scent becomes specific because it makes us feel different. I will illustrate this idea with a short story.

When I was a freshman in high school I played football for the first time. After the first day of practice we were allowed to take home our practice jersey. A few days later I hung out with a girl whom I had recently met. She had asked to wear my football jersey and later that night we kissed, which for me was a big deal. The girl was cute and I was inexperienced, so I felt excited, anxious, and proud. As it turned out, the scent of my football jersey eventually became associated with sensual excitement and the images of that girl. Whereas it is likely that my teammates had jersey associations related to grass fields, sweat, locker room, or other such impressions. Although, who knows, perhaps they had their own peculiar football jersey scent images? "Smell is always of something," Hillman (1979a) reminds us, "so imagining is always held within the bounds of a specific image" (p. 142). In any case, my story reflects how emotions experienced within a certain context are key elements in how scents become particularized.

Research in the natural sciences proposes at least two aspects that make olfaction unique among our senses. The first is that our experience with odors are idiosyncratic, and the second, that our verbal and written descriptions of scents are likewise peculiar.

Part of the reason our experiences with odors are idiosyncratic is due to how we take in sensory stimuli. "The person-to-person variability in odor perception is enormous," points out Gilbert (2008, p. 233). Why some people are able to smell particular odor molecules and others not, or why some find an aroma pleasurable and others not is still a mystery for scientists. "Idiosyncratic experiences with odors are a primary cause for unexpected aromatic reactions," claims Herz (2009). "Any given individual within a specific culture may not have the predicted response to an odor due to their own personal associations" (p. 283). Or more generally, take, for instance, W.H. Auden's (1962) observation: "Many of us have sacred landscapes which probably all have much in common, but there will almost certainly be details which are peculiar to each" (p. 56). It is clear that our personal associations with odors, as well as our emotions, are key elements in determining why our experiences with odors are primarily idiosyncratic in nature.

Next, we noted that the verbal and written accounts of odor experiences are peculiar and specific. "The way people describe odors is quite idiosyncratic compared with their description of colors, because description of odors is influenced more by individual experiences than by inherent neurophysiological processes" (Engen, 1982, p. 172). One of my favorite ways of observing the peculiar (and sometimes hilarious) way people have of describing odors and taste is to read beer and wine reviews. I will give an example from an international website called RateBeer.com. This is one man's description of a beer named Aunt Sally, from Lagunitas Brewery in southern California: "Yellow with a white head. Smells like lemon detergent and sadness. The flavor is horrid. A combo of rotten lemons and Pledge. I can't wait for this to be over." Lemon detergent and sadness! Who else would put those two words together to describe the aroma of a beer? In contrast, here is another description of the same beer:

"Nose is faintly sour, citrus. Unique taste profile...it is a soft bitter lemon, a little bit of peel, a backdrop of cake. Palate...definite body, chewiness. Overall, it has tart lemon cake profile with a nice body." Whereas the first person noted a lemon scent mixed with cleaning detergent, the second reviewer smells lemon combined with cake. Same exact beer—very different feelings, words, and images described by two people.

The idiosyncratic nature of scent experiences and subsequent responses leads me to wonder if it is even possible--or desirable—to speak in generalities about scent images. Even such a common American aroma of, let's say, buttered popcorn, will likely evoke different images for different people. "Even the most innocuous scent becomes objectionable if it reminds us of an unpleasant experience," notes Gilbert (2008, p. 114). Buttered popcorn could evoke images that range from banal movie theater experiences, to fond images of childhood sleepovers, to violent hatred as one experiences images of one's abusive father throwing popcorn on the floor.

We must therefore start with specifics rather than with generalizations or boxing scent experiences into categories and types. Berry (2008) summarizes our starting point: "We, as craftsmen or artists of the psyche, begin with distinct, particular perceptions rather than with generalities into which particulars must then fit...We encourage the aesthetic perception of particulars in lieu of global thinking" (pp. 172-173). This is not to say that there is anything wrong with speaking in generalities, but in the case of scent images, generalizing or typing will not sufficiently illuminate our olfactory experience.

Hillman (1977) makes a strong statement about generalities when he writes, "Images that are generalized and conventionalized have had their characteristic peculiarity erased. They no longer can rightly be called images" (p. 66). Hillman is highlighting the importance of the idiosyncratic image, but when it comes to scent images, I believe that generalities are the exception rather than the rule; it is not easy to find common or general scent images. Therefore, the precision of the scent image is vital. "Precision means whatever is actually presented. Simply: the actual qualities of the image" (p. 69). It is the details of the image that catch our attention, or rather should be given more attention. A common perfume from Macy's may be inconsequential for one person, but for another, multiple images of his ex-wife may thrust themselves into consciousness upon inhaling the perfume: her smile, her caress, or the squint in her eyes just before she asked for a divorce. "Nothing in general is really threatening," writes Berry (2008). "Only the specific and the unexpected hit us hard" (p. 174). We are often hit hard by the idiosyncratic image. Note how this idea is also related to the previous qualities of scent images: that they evoke and are emotional and embodied.

It is a natural part of the human mind to try and simplify our experiences. We therefore make use of abstractions, categories, and types to organize and consolidate the immense data that we have internalized. Yet we must resist this temptation to speak in general categories when investigating the soul and its scent images. In order to do this, we must give each evocative scent impression its due attention. Hillman (1975) elaborates:

> To see what a thing is requires a fresh perception
> for each image, whereas types conveniently mold
> everything into their own image. Only the image
> can free us from typecasting, since each image has
> its particular peculiarity that fits no preconceived
> frame. (p. 144)

To be able to see each image with a fresh perception we would do well to tune in to our somatic sensations and our emotions. When it comes to perceptual scent images we might pay attention to the colors of the new food dish we are eating or the music that is playing in the back of the restaurant. When a memory image is involved we could feel the sense of lightness or heaviness in our body, for instance. This simple move will add texture to the scent image. Paying attention to a couple details will typically engender more images. Bachelard (1943/1988) proclaims that, "if an image does not determine an abundance—an explosion—of unusual images, then there is no imagination. There is only perception, the memory of a perception" (p. 1).

If we are stimulated by an odor of hairspray, for instance, we may notice our nose stinging, our chest constricting, and perhaps pressure in our temples. We would then pay attention to the details of the psychic image presenting itself: feelings of anger and resentment as scenes come into focus of a former co-worker whom we once had a fight with. You see her wearing large, silver hoop earrings and emitting an odor of cheap hairspray. Rather than dismiss the images and feelings, we may pause and focus in on what has presented itself. Berry (2008) offers a suggestion on how we may better notice particular scents: "What is required is a sharp eye to situation—the shape of the work, the behavior, the action, the feeling within a particular context" (p. 172). In other words, to avoid types and generalities we need to pay attention to the context of the scent image—all the details of place, people, and emotions. Russell Lockhart (1987) stresses the personal significance that detailed images engender:

> In the same way that we often tend to overlook the intimate details of a mythic story by pulling out only a thread or two from an exceedingly interwoven fabric, we likewise overlook many details of imagery that are "unrecognizable" in the pattern and unique in their quality. Often we are more attracted to the details of imagery that can be readily comprehended, referred to known aspects of a known context, where we can quickly rush into a kind of settledness. What gets overlooked and quickly forgotten is the fine and subtle detail that is unique—absolutely unique. Yet one's exact fate and individuality are tied to those details. (p. 54)

It is probable that an idiosyncratic scent image is less likely to be dismissed or forgotten than other images, simply because it is so peculiar to us. It is as if the details of our scent images cannot help but capture our attention, as if the particulars were themselves alive. "Living images are highly idiosyncratic and psychoactive, meaning that they stimulate distinct physical and emotional responses" (Coppin & Nelson, 2005, p. 64). Perhaps Lockhart would agree that it is the details of our images that are keeping us alive. That is, it is those particular images that keep us engaged with life, make us feel deeply, and fulfill our inherent need for beauty. "The soul does not want mere recollection, literalism, or certainty; it wants living images full of emotion; it wants art that evokes these emotions," writes Lyn Cowan (2002, p. 62). I would argue that the soul not only wants art, but also wants aromas that likewise evoke, fragrances that move us emotionally. The soul wants scent images that are alive, for these living images remind us that we are beautifully and painfully alive. As Hillman (1975) insightfully writes:

> "Know thyself" means also know thy peculiar images, holding them in an interior void, close and familiar, without doing anything to them or for them. It is an inactive imagination and sometimes this is enough, for as we put events inside to carry and hold and digest, space is created to contain them. (pp. 93-94)

We may not have a large quantity of scent images, but the ones we do have are rich in particulars and are peculiar to us, and we do indeed need psychic space to contain them. They need to be contained because they want to stay with us; our scent images intend to stick around.

The Sticking of the Image

Caught up in contemplation, the mind's eye
Fixed upon images that once were thought,
For perfected, completed, and immovable
Images can break the solitude
Of lovely, satisfied, indifferent eyes.
~W.B. Yeats, *"The Phases of the Moon"*

Arrive then, son of darkness and stench!
How firmly you cling to the rubble
and waste of the eternal cesspit!
~C.G. Jung, *Liber Novus*

We started our investigation on the making of a scent image and have so far presented three factors or qualities in the construction of scent images, namely, the evocative, emotional-embodied, and idiosyncratic. I will now turn to the fourth characteristic of a scent image: its stickiness. Hillman (2016d) maintains that the arrival of an image not only strikes us, but that it also sticks. "Suddenly you get a tune in your mind, you see a girl on the street, you remember something that happened that you had forgotten for forty-seven years—and this strikes you and sticks" (p. 407). Hillman is maintaining that the initial recognition of the image is influenced by the way in which the image presents itself to our awareness. Not only must the image arouse us, perturb or stimulate, it must also adhere. Let us recall the idea of the psychic threshold and the need for sensory stimuli to be strong enough to break through into consciousness. We can observe that even if a sense impression is strong enough to evoke an emotional response, we cannot properly receive it if it rapidly leaves our awareness. If the impression does not stick or stay with us it will likely be dismissed by our ego and no image will form. On the other hand, if we recall the existence of the unconscious, we must allow for the possibility of image formation with minimal to no conscious awareness. In this case the initial scent image will make its presence known at a future time when it surfaces in our awareness as an implicit memory image.

This idea will be taken up further in the next chapter on memory. Now, let us observe, for instance, this passage from Helen Keller (2009):

> Once, long ago, in a crowded railway station, a lady kissed me as she hurried by. I had not touched even her dress. But she left a scent with her kiss which gave me a glimpse of her. The years are many since she kissed me. Yet her odor is fresh in my memory. (p. 30)

To me this is a perfect example of a scent image because it sticks. Keller's experience of being kissed by an unknown woman stayed with her for many years. The only sensory stimuli she had were the kiss and the accompanied scent of the woman, but it was enough to give Keller a "glimpse" of her. This turned out to be an image that many years later she could still recall. Was the persistence of the image due to how the memory was acquired, or was it the result of the quality of the scent itself? We do not know from this passage what Keller's emotions and thoughts were at the time of the experience, but we would not be too far off the mark if we assumed that Keller's kiss experience was highly emotional and arousing. This assumption is based upon research which has demonstrated that the formation of vivid scent memories is usually accompanied by strong emotions (Herz, 2007, 2016). My guess is that the stickiness of the image was the result of a particular context, i.e., a combination of somatic sensations, emotional feelings, as well as the quality of the scent itself. In any case, a scent image was formed and clearly stuck with her.

As we have noted throughout this chapter, emotions play a vital role in the evocativeness and stickiness of the scent image. "We may have only a vague, fleeting memory of the literal circumstances of a long-past event, but the emotions attached to that wisp of memory are still sharp, piercing, lodged permanently and precisely in the imagination and in the body" (Cowan, 2002, pp. 63-64). For example, I recall the first time my school bus began picking up kids from the campground to take us to elementary school. The few kids who got on the bus smelled like they had slept the night in rotten Rosemary bushes or something. I recall the odor gave me a headache and I had to plug my nose. After school I asked my mom why the kids at the campground smelled the way they did; it was a new smell for me. I learned that it was because they were likely poor and that the campground is where they lived, and possibly did not shower daily. Thus, to my initial feelings of disgust by their scent were now added feelings of pity, sadness, and compassion for them. I remember the first couple hours after arriving to school, the scent images of the campground kids remained with me. It was as if the odor molecules were lodged in my nostrils. As an interesting side note, Herz (2007) maintains that "molecules we can smell are chemically sticky; they literally stick to paint, cloth, and plastics" (p. 236)—and to our nostrils? The point of my school bus experience is to illustrate how strong emotions may contribute to the stickiness of a scent image.

Following Hillman's notion that images stick, Casey adds: "The French have the idea of *L'image obsessionnelle*...it overcomes you, it directs you; you don't direct it, it directs you" (as cited in Hillman, 2016d, p. 407). Obsessed by the image, unable to let it go. A scent image that remains fresh and poignant, despite its unpleasantness, is experienced by Rostov, one of the protagonists in Leo Tolstoy's (2007) great novel, *War and Peace*:

> Rostov stood at that corner for a long time, watching the feast from a distance. In his mind, a painful process was going on which he could not bring to a conclusion. Terrible doubts rose in his soul. Now he remembered Denisov with his changed expression, his submission, and the whole hospital, with arms and legs torn off and its dirt and disease. So vividly did he recall that hospital stench of dead flesh that he looked round to see where the smell came from. (p. 1,281)

Rostov could not bring to conclusion the stench of death and the associated war images; he was overcome with horrible scenes which overpowered him. We may conjecture that the odor of dirt, disease, and death remain so vivid for Rostov because of the associated emotionality in which the images inhered. To see one's comrades with their limbs severed has to be extremely upsetting. Yet perhaps there is a reason certain images obsess? It is as if repetitive polishing of the image, even if it disturbs us, somehow enriches the psyche. In Hillman's (1983a) view:

> Follow what the psyche itself does…a demand for details, precision. To get the image precise by worrying it, by going over it a thousand times…the psyche constructs, like a jeweler, a watchmaker, in this obsessional way. It's making an image of the event. (p. 23)

Because scents are typically fleeting and transitory, it is all the more fascinating when a scent image becomes obsessive. "Images hold us; we can be in the grip of an image. Indeed they can be gusty" (Hillman, 1978, p. 159). Even with the greatest of willpower some scent images will not depart from our awareness easily. In the novel, *The Damned*, by J. K. Huysmans (2002), the character Durtal is obsessed with a woman:

> If you knew how much I have thought about you! Now I have you here, all to myself, and he spoke of that persistent odour of cinnamon, faint, distant, expiring amid the less definite odours which her gloves exhaled, "well," and he sniffed her fingers, "you will leave some of yourself here when you go away." (p. 315)

Durtal admits his obsession to the woman and then alludes to further obsessions with her scent in the future. Later in the scene Durtal tries to seduce her, but unsuccessfully. He probably should have just kept to his fantasies of her rather than act them out. Or perhaps he should have taken Bachelard's (1943/1988) advice and "abandon what we see or what we say in favor of what we imagine. In this way we may be able to reinvest the imagination with its role as seducer" (p. 3). This literary example may be stretching the "stickiness of the image" idea, but I simply wish to emphasize that there are reasons why some scents stick around in our psyches, and that the stickiness contributes to the making of a scent image.

A final example I will offer that demonstrates the extreme stickiness of an image comes from a short story by D. H. Lawrence (1965):

> He went through the morning's affairs drunk with anger and suppression. In his mind was one thing—Banford. He took no heed of all March's outpouring: none. One thorn rankled, stuck in his

> mind. Banford. In his mind, in his soul, in his whole being, one thorn rankling to insanity. (p. 167)

The image that sticks for the character in Lawrence's novel is not of a scent but of a person named Banford. The important point I want to make is that the image felt like a thorn, and unable to let go the image of Banford, the character feels he is heading toward insanity. Extreme emotions and an image that cannot be dismissed would leave us all a little insane.

Yet is there something more than the evocative, emotional, embodied, and idiosyncratic nature of images that makes them stick? In Casey's (1974a) view, "what cannot be imagined away is the essence or *eidos* within the image that 'keeps intruding itself'" (p. 29). To know what the essence within the image entails, we must be willing to go into the image deeply. Not so much with philosophical why questions, or scientific how questions, but rather with what questions (Hillman, 1975, p. 138). What is there in the image, presented to us in all its strangeness and beauty? We are called upon to survey the landscape of the image—the smellscape—in all its details and particulars, which include not only scents, but also sights, sounds, and touch impressions. For as we shall see next, scents are never alone. So, to know the essence of the image we must have a starting place from which to enter the smellscape. As Hillman writes, "Poets wait for a line to come, from which they can go on working, or a little melody is picked up in a bird's song, or a striking image comes and sticks with you, that's the beginning" (Shamdasani & Hillman, 2013, pp. 47-48).

Scents Are Never Alone

*What would odors signify if they were not
associated with the time of the year,
the place I live in,
and the people I know?*
~Helen Keller, *The World I Live In*

*On my breathing the stars rise and set.
At my lips fragrances come to drink,
and I recognize the wrists of distant angels.*
~R. M. Rilke, *"The Silence"*

Although my research concentrates on olfaction
and the human psyche, it is important to acknowledge that
olfaction cannot ever be studied or experienced in
isolation. There are two primary reasons why "scents are
never alone." The first has to do with nouns (objects,
people, etc.), the second deals with our other sensory
modalities (sight, sound, touch, taste) and the phenomena
of *synesthesia*.

First, scent molecules must emanate from
something or someone. "An odor is only an attribute of
something else: an object, another person, an event, a
certain environment. To the extent that these things are
distinctive, their odors are distinctive. The odors are
henceforth recognized because of their associations with
things" (Engen, 1991, p. 87). For example, we cannot
smell exhaust fumes without an automobile, boat, or plane
to produce it. Olfaction therefore does not occur in
isolation; source objects and place are always involved
and can easily overlap with other scent objects. Clare
Batty (2010) offers this perspective:

We never, on the basis of olfactory experience
alone, differentiate where certain olfactory
property is instantiated and where it is not. Doing
so involves the contribution of movement and,
quite possibly, input from the other sensory
modalities. For example, a sighted person will rely
on visual experience to trace where the source of
the smell is, to determine where the smell is
strongest, weakest and where it simply is not. This
kind of investigation occurs through time. We get
up, move around, sniff, foot by foot, room by
room. We navigate the olfactory terrain; we
actively engage in figuring out where the smells
are located in the space around us. (pp. 523-524)

Even if we cannot locate the source of an odor, we know it must come from something or someone; a smell cannot exist on its own. Porteous (1985) elaborates this idea in reference to smellscapes. "Many smells provide little information about the location of their source in space. Yet it is common experience that smells are not randomly distributed, but are located with reference to source, air currents, and direction from source" (pp. 359-360). Thus, we can see how smells always have a referent; they cannot be experienced otherwise.

Moreover, from a depth psychological perspective, the same can be said of scent images within the psyche. "Smell is always of something, so imagining is always held within the bounds of a specific image—this image, right here, under your nose" (Hillman, 1979a, p. 142). Can a scent that reaches the ego be experienced without a mental reference or image to something, even if the odor is unknown? Hillman (1979a) would most likely answer no. "Smells cannot stand alone. They must be linked to an image: rose-odor, toast-scent, refinery-stench" (p. 140). The term ego written above is in keeping with Jung's idea: "The portion of the psyche made up of easily accessed thoughts, memories, and feelings at whose center is the ego, the 'I'" (as cited in Stein, 2015, p. 233). However, many scents do not reach the ego and are therefore not experienced as a psychic image directly. Nevertheless, scents that do not reach the ego are still not neglected or alone, in the sense that the unconscious psyche does in fact receive them. "Some odors are conspicuous, but that is not required for the formation of memories. Odor associations can be formed automatically and without conscious awareness" (Engen, 1991, p. 6).

The second aspect of olfactory relatedness: "The sense of smell does not exist in isolation," notes Engen (1991), "but is intimately related to other modalities and is influenced by their inputs, including temperature and even motor activity in chewing food" (p. 93). The close connection between taste and smell is a clear example. For instance, "flavor is actually a fusion of taste and smell," points out Gilbert (2008, p. 92). "Because smell and taste are inextricably linked in flavor perception, experience in one modality can affect the other" (p. 94). We know that if our nose is plugged up our taste experience is reduced or diminished. Children (and some adults) naturally pinch their nostrils if they have to ingest nasty tasting food, drink, or medicine.

Conversely, sniffing food or drink before we ingest it to enhance the flavor is not uncommon. Perhaps we do this because "odor contributes to taste intensity" (Engen, 1982, p. 154). For me, the enjoyment (and obsession) of taking several sniffs before a delicious meal adds another sensuous layer to my dining experience; in anticipation of a fabulous dish I stick my face close to the food, sniffing, lingering more than is socially common. In the case of high quality, aromatic beers, I prefer to pour it into a tulip glass, which has a wide rim to allow my nose full access to the aromas. Before any beer touches my lips, my nose greedily drinks in the fragrance. Wine connoisseurs do this too, of course, swirling and sniffing before sipping. Thus, "even at the simplest perceptual level, an odor is not a singular, isolated sensory event but one intimately associated with other sensory stimulation, especially that from gustatory and trigeminal activation" (Engen, 1991, p. 111). Other researchers note that, "our odor perception is more holistic than analytic" (Royet et al., 2013, p.2). It seems to me that what these scientists are alluding to is the experience of synesthesia, the blending of the senses, where *syn* (together) combines with *aisthanesthai* (to perceive) or *aisthesis* (sensation)—to perceive or sense together (Ackerman, 1990, p. 289).

However, synesthesia is often defined as the stimulation of one modality leading to a sensation in another modality. For example, "a sound may be experienced as a green color" (Engen, 1982, p. 153). Because it may seem strange to hear someone say he can taste the color blue, synesthesia is often considered a neurological "abnormality." However, upon close examination, synesthesia is not an abnormality, but is actually reflective of our lived experience. Philosopher and ecologist David Abram (1996) explains:

> Our primordial, preconceptual experience, as Merleau-Ponty makes evident, is *inherently*

> synaesthetic. The intertwining of sensory
> modalities seems unusual to us only to the extent
> that we have become estranged from our direct
> experience (and hence from our primordial contact
> with the entities and elements that surround us)
> …this is not to deny that the senses are distinct
> modalities. It is to assert that they are divergent
> modalities of a single and unitary living body, that
> they are complementary powers evolved in
> complex interdependence with one another. Each
> sense is a unique modality of this body's existence,
> yet in the activity of perception these divergent
> modalities necessarily intercommunicate and
> overlap. (pp. 60-61)

The overlap of our divergent modalities is seen clearly in
our common language. Helen Keller (2009) noticed this
when she wrote:

> People who have five senses find it difficult to
> keep their functions distinct. I understand that we
> hear views, see tones, and taste music. I am told
> that voices have color. Tact, which I had supposed
> to be a matter of nice perception, turns out to be a
> matter of taste. (p. 19)

In short, we must always keep in focus that scents are
never experienced in isolation. As Rodaway (1994) points
out, "olfactory geographies are quite complex, including
reference to relationships between sources and effects,
across time and space" (p. 65). Aromas therefore cannot
be written or spoken about without reference to objects,
places, persons, and our other senses. They are relational
and synesthetic in the sense that they both influence and
interpenetrate other facets of our world. Thus, the scent

images that arrive in our psyches are always situated within a particular context. It is toward this varied and fragrant landscape that we now turn.

Outer Smellscapes

Landscape images hold memories
that tell stories.
~James Hillman, *Landscape*

Someone in charge would give up all his power,
If he caught one whiff of the wine-musk
from the room where the lovers
are doing who-knows-what
~Rumi, *The Essential Rumi*

Douglas Porteous, a geography professor and author, first introduced the term *smellscape* in 1985. As a cultural-conceptual tool it offered another way to investigate olfaction (Rindisbacher, 2015, p. 81). Porteous' (1985) intention was to "pioneer the exploration of the landscape of smell," within the context of "person, place, and time" (p. 357). As Rindisbacher also notes, the "*idea* and the *concept* of something like an 'olfactory landscape' signaled that smells were beginning to be envisioned as a *field* in cultural and historical research" (2015, p. 81). This is important because it marked a shift away from, or an addition to, traditional biochemical or psychophysical olfactory research. Porteous explains the smellscape in this way:

> The concept of the smellscape suggests that, like visual impressions, smells may be spatially ordered

> or place related. It is clear, however, that any
> conceptualization of smellscape must recognize
> that the perceived smellscape will be non-
> continuous, fragmentary in space and episodic in
> time. (1985, p. 359)

Instead of focusing on one particular scent, our orientation toward the smellscape would require us to pay attention to the multiple and diverse aromas in the external environment that are available to the perceiving soma. In other words, we are in the realm of "the empirical world of determinate loci in an objective space and time" (Casey, 1974a, p. 25). However, this may be difficult to do analytically, notes Gilbert (2008). "We do a better job of collecting smells than we do of tracking them in a complex mixture…the problem is not in the nose but in the brain. We have limited ability to think about smells analytically" (p. 24).

Thus, if our brain is limited in its ability to track different aromas and think about them analytically, perhaps we should tune into scents imagistically. Less analysis, more images. We likewise would do well to take advantage of our intelligent bodies to "collect smells," so to speak. In other words, we should use our felt sense in our vibrating somas to participate in the smellscape.

But the empirical world, as Descartes once proclaimed, is not simply full of dead objects, an unfeeling smellscape as it were. No, "innate to the landscape are the emotions we feel in a landscape's presence," Hillman (2016a) reminds us, "and these moods and feelings are not merely in our brains, our heart, our senses…there is also an objective subjectivity afforded by the scene and inherent to it" (pp. 360-361). In other words, not only can we notice the variety of aromas in the environment but we can also recognize that scents of a given area belong to that place. For instance, the northern California coastal town of Santa Cruz has a remarkable combination of odors than differs from my hometown of Carpinteria in southern California. Santa Cruz has sharp, clean-smelling air that is infused with Redwood forest scents along with colder water and more sea kelp, which seems to produce a stronger "sea smell." Carpinteria on the other hand has drier air, dust from the freeway, and offshore oil platforms which contributes a salty-tar odor to the sea shore. Thus, the scents of both towns are as much a part of their community as are the people, buildings, and topography.

Furthermore, we participate in their field, their smellscape. "If in some sense the world imprints itself on our minds, it is equally true that our experiences are imprinted on the world," writes Paul Auster (as cited in Hillman, 2016a, p. 363). Just as our water and soil absorb chemicals from human activity, perhaps the land also takes in our feelings, thoughts, and images. This view is contrary to materialistic and Cartesian notions that consider outer tangible reality and inner states of mind to be opposed or separate. "We have lost the third, middle position," argues Hillman (1975, p. 68). That middle position, as we have already touched upon, is the soul, or the dynamic imaginal realm.

In the same way we take in all the visual objects near and far or tune in to all the sounds of a given place, so too we take in the "enveloping, unstructured, often directionless space" (Porteous, 1996, p. 36) in which we experience the world's fragrances. Porteous is describing our exterior environment as it is permeated with scents.

However, Paul Rodaway (1994), in his book *Sensuous Geographies: Body, Sense, and Place* considers Porteous' idea of smellscape as too ambiguous, passive, and limited, and instead uses "olfactory geography" (pp. 62-63). He is critical of the term smellscape because:

> [It] fails to genuinely reflect the everyday nose-experience of a world around us. Smells do not offer scenes or views, objects arranged and set at a distance from the observer. Rather, smells are present or not present, in varying degrees of intensity and subject to the movement of air (or the locomotion of our bodies through space). Smells infiltrate or linger, appear or fade, rather than take place or situate themselves as a composition. (p. 64)

Rodaway's criticism is warranted if we take olfaction literally and expect our scent experiences to behave like our visual ones. But smells do not and cannot "situate themselves as a composition" in the same way objects in our visual field do. If Rodaway were less literal in his thinking he could understand how smells can be part of imaginative scenes, psychic images as if the smell were an object of optical apperception. The "as if" stance helps us de-literalize scents solely as external objects and instead welcomes the "ambiguous" smellscape into our experience. Moreover, the concept of the smellscape "both in concrete spatial terms and ideationally, provides shape and coherence to real-world olfactory phenomena" (Rindisbacher, 2015, p. 81); the smellscape gives us a container, a theater in which to situate ourselves in the world of fragrances.

Of the numerous examples of the outer smellscape, I am drawn to a section of D. H. Lawrence's (2009) novel, *Mornings in Mexico*:

> There is a little smell of carnations, because they are the nearest thing. And there is a resinous smell of ocate wood, and a smell of coffee, and a faint smell of leaves, and of Morning, and even of Mexico. Because when all is said and done, Mexico has a faint, physical scent of her own, as each human being has. And this is a curious, inexplicable scent, in which there are resin and perspiration and sun- burned earth and urine among other things. (p. 10)

This is a fine description of diverse aromas situated both within the immediate surroundings of the narrator, as well as other scents encountered throughout the country. Without ever having been to Mexico, the reader, through use of the smellscape, can easily situate himself in a concrete place, one that is well shaped and accessible to the imagination.

I will therefore use the term smellscape in my research on meaningful scent images because the idea and concept of the smellscape is a practical term for encapsulating the multiple aromas in the external environment. I have added the seemingly redundant "outer" to smellscapes so that I may contrast it with an "inner" smellscape, such as I will describe below.

I want to point out an important idea before I differentiate "outer" and "inner" smellscapes. The apparent separation between inner and outer is, in my view, an illusion or a mistake in thinking. "There is an inexhaustible ocean of likenesses between the world within, and the world without," points out Keller (2009, p. 56). With only a simple investigation we can understand how it is impossible to speak or write about the odors of a given landscape without a perceiving human subject, a pulsing, breathing soma who is sensing and perceiving the various odorants. Likewise, the inner smellscape (psychic images) cannot be separated from environmental stimuli (outer smellscape) that combine to form a complex and dynamic psychic reality. John Macy (1877-1932), Helen Keller's friend and original biographer, describes how external stimuli and the imagination interpenetrate:

> Miss Sullivan, who knows her pupil's mind, selects from the passing landscape essential elements, which give a certain clearness to Miss Keller's imagined view of an outer world that our eyes is confused and overloaded with particulars. If her companion does not give her enough details, Miss Keller asks questions until she has completed the view to her satisfaction. (Keller, Sullivan, Macy, Shattuck, & Herrmann, 2003, p. 221)

Despite being blind and deaf, Keller is able, with the help of her teacher, to construct a picture of reality that is rich with images, a smellscape that is both external and internal. Hillman (1975) elaborates on this illusion between interior and exterior:

> We live in a world that is neither 'inner' nor 'outer.' Rather the psychic world is an imaginal world, just as image is psyche. Paradoxically, at the same time these images are in us and we live in the midst of them. The psychic world is experienced empirically as inside us and yet it encompasses us with images. (p. 23)

Hillman was influenced by and took some of his ideas of the imagination (including the word "imaginal") from Islamic scholar, Henry Corbin (1972). *Mundus Imaginalis,* one of Corbin's oft-cited works have elements of relevance here. Corbin, quoting Sadra Shirazi, writes: "Whereas in the outer world there are five sensible faculties, each with its specific organ in the body, in the *inner world* they are *synthesized* into one" (p. 13). It is as if the imaginal world makes use of all available sensory impressions yet is less concerned with literalisms and the need to sharply differentiate concrete images from abstract or fantasy images. In other words, we are moving intimately between worlds, back and forth, from scent images without to scent images within.

Inner Smellscapes

Take in the color and perfume of phenomena
and the five inner senses open onto the mystery
~Rumi, *The Essential Rumi*

A whiff of perfume, or even the slightest
odor can create an entire environment
in the world of the imagination.
~Gaston Bachelard, *The Poetics of Space*

Nowhere, beloved, can world be but within us.
Our life passes in transformation.
And the external dwindles away.
Where a house stood and endured,
now it will move across consciousness as image
~R. M. Rilke, *"The Seventh Elegy"*

If the outer smellscape is the totality of aromas in the external environment available to the perceiving subject, then the inner smellscape is comparable to the psyche itself, an interior world full of dynamic sense impressions and living images. Casey (1974b) uses the phrase "imagined world-frame" to encapsulate this idea. He summarizes thus:

> The full imagined content includes not only particular objects and/or states of affairs, but also their immediately surrounding context. We may call this contextual factor "the imagined world-frame of quasi-space and time." Since it is a matter of the experiential field within which imagined objects and states of affairs appear. (p. 10)

What Casey terms the "world-frame" may be analogous to what I am calling the "inner smellscape." Therefore, the inner smellscape can be viewed as a web of scent images, a constellation of aromas that are linked with emotions, objects, people, and which are situated within particular contexts of time and space. In this sense the inner smellscape will always include some part of the outer smellscape. Rachel Herz (2007) offers an excellent description of the inner smellscape:

> What we think a certain scent is, its connection to language and concept, what the scent means to us, what it makes us feel, and what it reminds us of— all interact in a complex multifaceted dance and determine our *perception* of that scent. Odor sensation happens at the level of our nose and olfactory bulb, but olfactory perception occurs in our mind, where our personal experiences with scents take over. (p. 29).

Herz says olfactory perception occurs in our mind, which in my view is only partially correct. I would argue that it is actually our psyche in which the "complex multifaceted dance" of perception occurs because the term psyche, as I have defined it, is more inclusive to our experience. It not only encompasses our conscious thoughts, memories, and feelings, but also those associations and feelings that are unconscious. Herz admits, "An association can be vague and you may only *feel* that a certain smell is good or bad, with no specific recollection in mind, but it can bring forth complex and intense personal memories" (p. 60). From where does the vague scent association with no specific memory arise? Jung (1961/1976) offers a fabulous example by telling a story of a professor walking in the country with a pupil, deep in serious conversation.

> Suddenly he notices that his thoughts are interrupted by an unexpected flow of memories from his early childhood. He cannot account for it, as he is unable to discover any associative connection with the subject of his conversation. He stops and looks back: there at a little distance is a farm, through which they had passed a short while ago, and he remembers that soon afterwards images of his childhood began to surge up. "Let us go back to the farm," he says to his pupil; "it must be about there that my fantasies started." Back at the farm, the professor notices the smell of geese. Instantly he recognizes it as the cause of the interruption: in his early youth he had lived on a farm where there were geese, whose characteristic smell had formed a lasting impression and caused the reproduction of the memory images. He had

> noticed the smell while passing the farmyard, subliminally, and the unconscious perception had called back long-forgotten memories. This example illustrates how the subliminal perception released early childhood memories, the energic tension of which proved to be strong enough to interrupt the conversation. The perception was subliminal because the attention was engaged elsewhere, and the stimulus was not strong enough to deflect it and to reach consciousness directly. Such phenomena are frequent in everyday life, but mostly they pass unnoticed. (p. 199)

Within the story that Jung describes are several key elements that we have been working upon in this chapter. First, the arrival of childhood memory images suddenly occurred. The man was assaulted by surging images, as it were, but he at first did not know the source of the evocation. An unconscious perception had taken place that had a strong enough energy charge to interrupt the man's thoughts. It was not until he smelled the geese that he made the association to his memory images. We do not know the emotional felt sense of the man, but we can assume that the smell of the geese stirred within the man feelings and emotions that were felt somatically. We also do not know how long the images stayed with the man, but since the story became "well-known" it is likely that the memory images and the scent stuck with him long enough for him to recount his story. Thus, we have a great example of an experience of the inner smellscape. The man encountered stimuli that was evocative, emotional, embodied, idiosyncratic (geese scent from a childhood farm), all of which stuck with him.

There are still further ways of describing the smellscape. Hillman (1975) used the phrase "imaginal geography" to differentiate the imagination into qualitative regions or of extending nonphysical space (p. 93). Casey (1974a) uses a similar term—*placescape*—in an attempt to map the imagination, which he says is "active and alive with archetypes" (p. 7). Helen Keller (2009) would agree with both Hillman and Casey:

> Without imagination what a poor thing my world would be! My garden would be a silent patch of earth strewn with sticks of a variety of shapes and smells. But when the eye of my mind is opened to its beauty, the bare ground brightens beneath my feet, and the hedgerow bursts into leaf, and the rose-tree shakes its fragrance everywhere. I know how budding trees look, and I enter into the amorous joy of the mating birds, and this is the miracle of imagination. (p. 4)

There is yet another way to look at the inner smellscape, this time from the perspective of neuroscience. Researchers Saive, Royet, and Plailly (2014) developed an "original laboratory-ecological approach" where participants explored three unique episodes over three days, which were each composed of three unfamiliar odors. These odors were positioned at three specific locations within a visual context. On the fourth day, the odors were used to trigger the retrieval of the complex episodes in a recall test. Their results demonstrated that the participants were "highly proficient in recognizing the target odors among distractors and retrieving the spatio-contextual environment of the episode with a rather high confidence level" (p. 8).

Based on their findings the researchers suggest that, "when an association between odors, spatial locations and contexts is encoded, the association forms an *integrated representation* [italics added] retrievable by the participants" (Saive et al., 2014, p. 8). The integrated representation includes the scent itself, the context in which the scent was experienced (this includes emotions, somatic sensations, people, objects, etc.), as well as any of the other four senses that may be involved. To me, the researchers are essentially describing the inner smellscape—a psychophysical experience that includes the external landscape in which the smell was encountered, as well as the internal images ("associations") that are "represented" within the psyche.

Now let us shift from neuroscience to literature and enter the inner smellscape of a character in D. H. Lawrence's (2009) short story, "Two Blue Birds":

> "I think," he began, "these are the loveliest afternoons, when there's no direct sun, but all the sounds and the colors and the scents are sort of dissolved, don't you know, in the air, and the whole thing is steeped, steeped in spring. It's like being on the inside; you know how I mean, like being inside the egg and just ready to chip the shell." (p. 117)

For the character in Lawrence's story, inner and outer realities have interpenetrated. The scents have been dissolved among other sensory impressions to form a felt sense of spring, of being enveloped within a unified field or integrated representation, as it were. Reading this passage, I feel as though I am more alive because my psyche has been aroused and transported into a smellscape of spring. Any reader can enter into that world. Likewise, our own inner smellscapes can become such a living reality, full of scenes, figures, textures, and of course scents, all of which provide nourishment for our soul.

Hillman reminds us that through the writing and publishing of *The Red Book*, Jung "reestablished that the psyche is a living world of imagination and that any person can descend into that world…that's what your soul is," and that this living world is figured, populated. "They are your teachers, they are your motivators, and they are your landscapes. That's what the habitations of your depths are" (Shamdasani & Hillman, 2013, p. 114). The inner smellscape: where we inhabit our depths of soul.

But within our soul depths we will inevitably come upon two forces that we must contend with: beauty and ugliness. "There is still a concern with the aesthetic," says Hillman (2016b) near the end of his life. "There is somehow a connection to beauty that has been lost: between the image world and the world of beauty" (p. 425). This leads me to think, what makes a scent image beautiful? What then also determines an ugly image? Casey responded to Hillman's concern with beauty:

> How is beauty carried, how is it presented? How is it carried forward? Or carried back, as you say, from another realm to this realm? Beauty could be a kind of superintending idea that would apply to each group of images: word images, painting images, you know, gesture images—my goodness, there is a whole world here. (as cited in Hillman, 2016b, p. 425)

To Casey I would answer, yes, beauty applies to scent images as well. To Hillman I would respond, no, we shall not lose our connection to beauty. The next chapter will concern itself with memory and the aesthetics of scent; there is a whole world there.

Chapter 4

THE GASP:
MEMORIES OF BEAUTY
AND DISGUST

The saffron spice of connecting, laughter
The onion smell of separation, crying
~Rumi, The Essential Rumi

I'm the rainbow in your jail cell
All the memories of everything
you've ever smelled
Not alone, I'll be there.
Tell me when you want to go
~Red Hot Chili Peppers, "Don't Forget Me"

For Remembrance, lifting her leanness,
keened in the gates of my heart
Till, fattening the winds of the morning,
an odour of new mown hay
Came, and my forehead fell low,
and my tears like berries fell down
~W.B. Yeats, "The Wanderings of Oisin"

I am standing in the back yard of a friend's house
party on a cool spring evening in southern Brazil, when a
woman slowly walks by me. I breathe in her scent. I gasp.
Nicole. She smells like Nicole! I feel my belly contract
slightly and my chest expand. I feel dizzy and euphoric at

the same time. I watch the woman, who I know not, disappear back inside the house. I feel my heart thumping and my legs seem unsteady, so I sit down in a chair near a small wood fire. My face feels flushed, though not from the fire. My eyes begin to sting and tear as strong emotions, along with hundreds of memories of my life with Nicole, implode upon me.

At the age of 23, not long after my first long-term romantic relationship of two years ended, I flew to Brazil for an extended stay. Part of my intention of going abroad was to heal from my relationship, of which the last six months together was one of the most difficult times in my life. The fresh culture of Brazil was for me a welcome relief. I heard different languages, saw new landscapes, and of course, was exposed to novel food and aromas. Thus it was a total surprise to catch a whiff of another woman who smelled like my former partner, whose scent I now cannot quite describe. "It is difficult to put into words the thing itself, the elusive person-odor. There seems no adequate vocabulary of smells," wrote Helen Keller (2009, p. 31). Her scent was not from an applied perfume either, but the unique and personal signature smell that I thought she alone emitted. I never imagined that her distinct smell that I knew intimately would exist anywhere or exude from anyone else. To be thousands of miles away and to suddenly inhale her scent left me awed and dismayed, aroused, and painfully nostalgic. I am reminded again of Helen Keller, who observed, "human odors are as varied and capable of recognition as hands and faces. The dear odors of those I love are so definite, so unmistakable, that nothing can quite obliterate them" (p. 30).

Part of me wanted to leave the party, another part of me wanted to ignore the scent and my stirring emotions, and just enjoy the social gathering. But I did neither. I sat a moment gazing into the fire and wondering if perhaps I had an olfactory hallucination, and that the woman who walked by didn't actually smell like Nicole, that my senses and my psyche made a mistake, or whether out of longing I projected her scent onto another woman. Despite the potential creepiness I might provoke, I felt drawn—compelled actually—to sniff that woman again.

I got up and went inside the house and eventually sighted the woman whose scent had unknowingly set me aflame. While her back was turned to me I glided past her on my way to the kitchen and was able to take one rapid and forceful inhale. No, it was not a hallucination. Her scent was unmistakable. With tears welling up again, I quickly returned to the fire outside. I spent the rest of the evening embraced in a vaporous fog of memories, images, and emotions of bittersweet nostalgia (or *saudades*, as the Brazilians frequently say to express a kind of nostalgia). I kept my belly tightened and my jaw clenched to hold back tears. When asked if anything was wrong with me, I told my friends I was just tired.

Despite the aromas from the wood fire, damp soil, wet grass, and beer, her scent seemed to linger in my nose for quite some time. It was as if my body and psyche were intent to hold on to an ancient relic of personal significance. Or maybe a part of me knew that the other woman's scent was the closest I would ever come to being intimate with Nicole again. Because it felt intimate indeed, like I had my face right against her face or neck. The scent, along with the accompanying nostalgia and sharp psychic images of two years together, enveloped me for the next few days. Bachelard (1960/1969) understood such longing: "The farther one is from his native land, the more he suffers from the nostalgia of its odors" (p. 139). I had not had such a powerful scent experience before that evening in Brazil and I have not had one since. Although after 12 years I cannot, at this moment, recall her unique scent, the smellscape of my psyche remains rich with details that began with one unexpected inhale.

The Gift and Burden of Language

The literary image puts words in motion;
It restores them to their imaginative function.
~Gaston Bachelard, *Air and Dreams*

Smells should be symbols par excellence.
~Dan Sperber, *Rethinking Symbolism*

When words run out we die.
~James Hillman, *You Taught Me Language*

My experience in Brazil of a scent-evoked memory reveals several elements that are important for my research into meaningful scent images. First, there was a surprising inhale of a familiar scent followed by memories, emotions, and somatic sensations. The scent was evocative, idiosyncratic, and it stayed with me for a while after. Now, in order for me to share this striking experience with others, it must be communicated in some way. Since my research method is hermeneutics, I am working within the domain of written language. If communicated correctly words can be a gift. Conversely, the struggle to find the right words to express our experiences can feel like a heavy burden. As I touched upon briefly in the preceding chapter, there are language difficulties regarding scents and olfaction. How do we describe scents in general? How do we write about scents that accurately reflect our experience with them? For, as Hillman (2016c) writes, "our language has an effect on the soul. So, our language must not merely speak of the soul (psychology) but speak to the soul" (p. 246). How do we explain what a scent does to our body and the emotions it stimulates? What are the words that will do justice to our rich inner smellscape? Finally, if we are to confess our most beautiful and disgusting scent memories, can we find the words that illuminate our souls' most meaningful scent experiences?

Before I dive into the topic of scent memories, I must put forth a conceptual framework for understanding how language has informed, and will continue to, inform and contain my research. This framework will involve a semantic system which is coded on one hand by sensations from concrete experience, and on the other by the psyche's use of metaphors and poetics.

Let us recall some observations and scientific findings about olfaction and semantics. Unlike sound and vision, odors have eluded human attempts to categorize and classify them. We are unable to designate precise, universal labels to scents, such as we have with the color spectrum (wavelength) for vision and quantifiable measurements (decibel) for sound (Engen, 1982, 1991; Rodaway, 1994). This is true at least for the English language—the one relevant for this study. "An odor does not elicit a universal name, as colors typically do. A different semantic system is involved," notes Engen (1991, p. 85). Also, "odors do not belong to classes determined by their chemical or physical attributes" (p. 117). Sperber (1975) takes this idea even further and asserts, "There is no semantic field of smells. The notion of smells only has as lexical sub-categories general terms such as 'stench' and 'perfume'" (p. 116). Clearly we do have a semantic field of smells, but one perhaps different from how we categorize our other senses. What is this semantic system to which Engen referred? Hillman (1979a) likens the semantics of scent to a parasite, meaning that scents do not have any language of their own, and therefore we must steal from our other senses or areas of experience (p. 140). Herz (2007) would agree with Hillman:

> In all languages that have been studied, there are fewer words that refer exclusively to the experience of fragrance than there are for any other sensation…more common terms like *floral* or *fruity* are references to the odor-producing objects (flowers and fruits), not the odors themselves. We also borrow terms from other senses–chocolate smells *sweet*, and grass smells *green*–to describe our aromatic encounters. (p. 58)

Whether we parasitically "steal" or kindly "borrow" terms from other senses, the point is that smells apparently cannot (semantically) stand on their own, and in order to speak or write about them we must incorporate other nouns, adjectives, and verbs into our semantic system. The problem is not one of inadequate vocabulary but of the inability to creatively use the words we already possess. "Terms and expressions are not lacking to designate smells, but they almost always do so in terms of their causes or their effects" (Sperber, 1975, p. 115). The causes to which Sperber is referring would be the source odorant (lexically primarily nouns) and the effect would be the feeling or somatic reaction to the odor (lexically primarily represented as adjectives and verbs). A few examples will be useful.

To creatively use nouns, we can call upon our wide range of experience with places, people, and objects. If we want to describe that a certain woman smelled "so good," it would be better to be specific and say she smelled sweet like a tuberose flower mixed with damp earth after a Hawaiian rain. If we choose to speak about automobile exhaust fumes, we could specify whether the scent was from a bus, big rig, or motorcycle, as they each smell a little different.

Adjectives are essential to describe both general and specific scent qualities and the feelings associated with their effects. Is the scent fresh or rancid, light or heavy, thick or wispy, putrid or clean? As Bachelard (1943/1988) writes, "when an adjective makes its object blossom, written poetry, the literary image, allows us to live slowly the time of its blooming" (p. 248). There are hundreds, perhaps thousands, of adjectives to choose from; it is a matter of using them imaginatively to make the object "bloom." Recall from my last chapter that words carry images as well as scents. Thus we are concerned here not only with practical, functional communication. "A language of images belongs less to communication than to imagination, less a rational device to be employed for certain effects than an experimental risk whose effects are unpredictable" (Hillman, 2016d, p.

42). It is an experimental risk indeed, but one that could prove to be rich, humorous, and more precisely reflect our soul's experience. For instance, we could say a beer smelled acidic, like someone urinated in a gym locker room and then cleaned it with a lemon-scented chemical solvent. Or the smell in the public bus was heavy and rough and made me feel dirty and sticky like a hot day at a dusty outdoor music festival. Note in these examples I also make use of similes (a type of metaphor) for figurative comparisons; describing one thing in terms of another engenders more images that help portray the feelings we are trying to express. I will discuss the use of metaphors more fully below.

Direct, strong, and active verbs are perhaps the most useful for olfactory semantics because of their versatility. For help with describing the source of smells we could use such verbs as burning, sweating, smoking, seeping, rotting, or baking. If we want to reveal what the smell itself is doing, we could say it is permeating, drifting, distracting, lingering, fleeting, or hinting. We may also say the scent is intruding into our nostrils or teasing and flirting us by its subtle and mild appearance.

To steal or borrow words from other senses would also go a long way toward assisting scents in their semantic deficiency. As I mentioned, the use of metaphors is especially effective in this regard. As Rindisbacher (2015) notes, "the good thing is that in literature, the very deficiencies encourage, in fact, require, linguistic creativity, generally of a metaphoric, quintessentially poetic type in metonymy and simile, when attempting to do justice to the complexities of, say, modern perfumery" (p. 84). We could write that a scent smelled bright and yellow or dark and brown. Or we may say a smell was loud or soft, discordant or melodic. Perhaps the scent was rough, smooth, cool, hot, slippery, jagged, or velvety. Note Herz's (2007) observation: "Almost all odors have a feel to them as well as a smell. For example, menthol feels cool and ammonia feels burning. What produces these feelings are the temperature, touch, and pain fibers of the trigeminal system in our face and nose" (p. 47). Of course, all the words we use for taste (which is derived primarily from smell) would be useful: bitter, pungent smells or salty, sweet, and bland scents.

Finally, we can make wise use of metaphors. Keller (2009) noted that "there seems to be no adequate vocabulary of smells, and I must fall back on approximate phrase and metaphor" (p. 31). This is important to understand because "our ordinary conceptual system, in terms of which we both think and act, is fundamentally metaphorical in nature" (Lakoff & Johnson, 1980, p. 3). I want to point out here that there are different kinds of metaphors (i.e. simile, analogy, illusion, etc.), and that I am using the word *metaphor* in the broadest sense here and throughout. For example, a smell may "stab me in the gut" or "drop me to my knees."

However, some thinkers directly oppose the idea that metaphors are fundamental to our reality. For instance, Richard Geldard (2000) writes, "the faculty of human understanding tends to the literal" (p. 69). But in the English language the use of metaphor is pervasive. "It is as though the ability to comprehend experience through metaphor were a sense, like seeing or touching or hearing, with metaphors providing the only ways to perceive and experience much of the world" (Lakoff & Johnson, 1980,

p. 239). Instead of saying a scent made me feel happy, I could say the aroma tickled my heart or gave me a warm hug. Metaphors make use of the fact that we borrow words from other senses. "The essence of metaphor is understanding and experiencing one kind of thing in terms of another" (p. 5). To put it differently we turn to Bachelard (1943/1988): "The *literary image* must be enriched with a new *oneirism*. Such is the dual function of the literary image: to mean something different and to make readers dream another way" (p. 249). Metaphors help us to dream another kind of dream.

But to make a scent metaphor effective we need the use of our imagination. "From the experientialist perspective, metaphor is a matter of imaginative rationality" (Lakoff & Johnson, 1980, p. 235). A description such as "her spicy scent lit my chest on fire and lifted me skyward with love wings" most likely appeals to our psyche more than "she smells sexy." As Bachelard (1943/1988) sharply points out, "the imagination is delighted by the literary image. Literature is not merely a substitute for some other activity. It brings a human desire to fruition. It represents an *emergence* of the imagination" (p. 249). It appears that our scent experiences coincide with our imagination and if we are skillful and creative with the use of metaphors, the images and feelings that we wish to express will be joyously fruitful.

The creative and imaginative use of language becomes all the more imperative when we notice the ease in which we use over-simplistic and dualistic words to describe our olfactory experiences. Much of what we read in olfactory research, as well as what we hear in common speech, revolves around pleasant/unpleasant scents, positive/negative or good/bad smells, etc. Notice this passage from Herz (2007): "Aromas people like elicit pleasant moods and have positive effects, while aromas people dislike tend to induce unpleasant moods and have negative or neutral effects" (p. 97). There is an ongoing debate about potential olfactory universals, which involve many different languages, so it makes sense to stick with simple dualistic terms. Besides, most people know whether they like a particular smell or not. Nevertheless, I suspect that the reason we typically resort to dualisms is that they simplify our experiences, which are actually quite complex. There is nothing wrong with this practical way of speaking. However, I also believe that phrases like, "there's a bad smell in my room," is partly due to cognitive and linguistic laziness and partly from lack of semantic practice.

Yet I am aware that I myself am using the dualistic terms beautiful/ugly, joyous/disgusting. I am choosing to do so for the sake of simplicity. However, I want to emphasize that these perceptions and emotions exist on a continuum and can also be mixed together. "The interpretation and hence experience of a scent is in the mind of the smeller," points out Herz (2007). "Fear, illness, happiness, and craving can be conjured from the very same aroma in the very same person" (p. 101). For instance, a scent memory might elicit feelings of disgust and anger, but may also evoke bittersweet nostalgia and melancholy. Such experiences are complicated and cannot be easily reduced to one or two words.

Hillman (1972) describes the psyche's voice as "a speech of ambiguities that is evocative and detailed, yet not definitive…a speech that leads to participation…. Such speech has impact because it carries body in it; it is speech alive" (p. 206). To create speech that is "evocative" and "alive" takes the sensibility of an embodied poetic imagination. Over-simplified descriptions of scent memories will not do justice to the psyche's complex and fluid nature. Rather, words that are dynamic, carry multiple meanings, and which provoke an emotional response are given higher regard. "My fingers are tickled to delight by the soft ripple of a baby's laugh," says Helen Keller (2009, p. 4).

We must, like Keller, take advantage of all our senses, all parts of speech—whatever we have at our disposal—to bring to life once again our psychic images that desire to be known and appreciated. For, as Bachelard (1943/1988) proclaims, "if words fail to evoke visual images, they lose some of their power. But words are the insinuation and fusion of images; they are not an even exchange for rigid concepts. They are fluid that moves our fluidic nature, a breath" (p. 98). It is our breath to which we now give attention, for to smell anything we must inhale, which is an organic, natural act of taking in, of gasping, a movement of aspiration and inspiration.

Aspiration and Inspiration

When memory breathes, all odors are good.
Great dreamers know how to breathe the past.
~Gaston Bachelard, *The Poetics of Reverie*

For our part, when we feel, we evaporate;
ah, we breathe ourselves out and away;
from ember to ember
we give off a fainter scent.
~R. M. Rilke, *"The Second Elegy"*

In the imaginary life of breath,
our soul is always our last sigh.
A bit of our soul joins a universal soul.
~Gaston Bachelard, *Air and Dreams*

An investigation of scent memories would not be complete if we did not mention the obvious: our breath. Whether we take deep and long inhales or a rapid burst of sniffs, to inhale is the only way we can smell anything. Plug our noses, and olfaction shuts down. But our breath is a curious phenomenon in that it is both voluntary and involuntary; we unconsciously always breathe but we have the ability to consciously alter our breath if we want. From birth to death the air we breathe is the one constant and "it is the air that most directly envelops us; the air, in other words, is that element that we are most intimately *in*" (Abram, 1996, p. 260). Since we are always breathing, we also always smell, though that too we are usually unconscious of. Scent molecules must make it far enough up the nose to be (even unconsciously) detected. "Smell— at least the first physiological contact with odor molecules–clearly happens in the nose. The holes in the cribriform plate are there to allow nerve fibers from the sensory cells to reach the brain" (Gilbert, 2008, p. 75). A way to get scent molecules further up the nasal passage is to sniff. "The sniff—a short inhalation with a high rate of airflow—is an essential step in odor detection. By forcing more air past the olfactory cleft, we take a bigger sample of the external smellscape" (p. 76).

To receive the world of fragrances we, like our animal cousins, sniff during all olfactory occasions. We sniff when we are unsure of an odor, when we want to take in more delicious aromas, or forcefully exhale when we want to expel horrid scents. "Sniffing is essential," writes Gilbert (2008). "Whether one is tracking down a dead mouse in the basement or savoring a newly opened bag of Doritos, the sniff is the prelude to a smell. The purpose of a sniff is to get the scent molecules to the place where we can smell them" (pp. 74-75). If a sniff is a prelude to a smell, then we can certainly say breathing is a prelude or prerequisite to the formation of a scent image and a scent memory; our breath is the beginning. Yet what about scent memories in the absence of an odorant (external stimulus), memories that reside solely within our imagination?

Observe this fascinating olfactory research statement: "So closely is sniffing tied to odor perception that people routinely sniff when they are asked to imagine a smell. Without prompting, they take longer sniffs when imagining pleasant odors and smaller ones when imagining malodors" (Gilbert, 2008, p. 81). It is as if our somatic memory of sniffing a past odor reawakens when our psyche consciously tries to recall the fragrance and the felt sense of a prior scent experience. Now, I close my eyes and return to the joyous smellscape of my childhood at my local beach. Yes, I do indeed tilt my head and nose up slightly and feel by belly and chest expand more fully as I breath deeper than I did just a minute ago. I even sniff a few times forcefully to expel more air, as I could feel a little sting in my nose from the salty sea breeze, tar, and mild fishy aroma. What I just described is apparently not an unusual act. "Sniffing at an imaginary odor isn't an absentminded habit—it's a behavior that improves the mental image we are trying to create," (p. 81) and "is critical to how we generate a mental image of the smellscape" (p. 84). That sniffing improves the mental image we are trying to create tells us about the powerful and vital role our breath plays in our psychic experience.

It is worth pointing out that in many cultures the words *breath*, *breathe* and *breathing* have linguistic roots in words that also mean soul and spirit. For instance, the ancient Greek word psyche "signified not merely the 'soul,' or the 'mind,' but also a 'breath,' or a 'gust of wind.' The Greek noun was itself derived from the verb *psychein*, which meant 'to breathe,' or 'to blow'" (Abram, 1996, pp. 237-238). As we considered in the last chapter, the psyche or soul is often seen as an intermediary, a third imaginal principal or metaphor between body and spirit, which Hillman (1979a) refers to as the *opus major*, "the grand conjunction of body, soul, and spirit." Hillman claims, "what holds that conjunction of concrete sensation, psychic image, and spiritual meaning is *aisthesis*, which denotes originally both breathing in (smelling) and perceiving" (p. 142). Inhalation, aspiration, sniffing—the great thread of the "opus major."

Thus we can understand the intimate connection between breath/air, psyche, and by extension, scent. Jung (1933/1969a) himself wrote of this idea:

> In Latin, Greek, and Arabic the names given to the
> soul are related to the notion of moving air, the
> 'cold breath of the spirits'…It is quite
> understandable that, since breath is the sign of life,
> it should be taken for life, as are also movement
> and moving force. (p. 345)

We could even go so far as to say that scent is another metaphor for the psyche itself. In fact, the ancient philosopher Heraclitus left us a couple fragments that allude to this possibility: "Soul is the vaporization out of which everything else is derived; moreover, it is the least corporeal of things and is in ceaseless flux, for the moving world can only be known by what is in motion," and "In Hades souls perceive by smelling" (as cited in Wheelwright, 1959, pp. 58-59). As we follow the thread of breath, life, and movement, let us observe the following passage from D. H. Lawrence (1961):

> What is the breath of life? My dear, it is the
> strange current of interchange that flows between
> men and men, and men and women, and men and
> things. A constant current of interflow, a constant
> vibrating interchange. That is the breath of life. (p.
> 116)

We breathe in the external smellscape, interiorizing its vibrating aliveness, as if having a lively conversation while sipping and smelling our coffee; and in another moment we exhale, offering back to the world our inner smellscape, each having been altered in the process. Likewise, we can close ourselves off to the world by plugging our nose. Sometimes this is desired and necessary; the external smellscape is filled with horrid aromas as much as it contains lovely ones. My English teacher in middle school had terrible breath that always smelled of old coffee and stale cigarettes. Her breath caused me to hold my breath whenever she leaned down to help me with my work. Nevertheless, like the somatic practitioner Ilse Middendor (1995) wrote, "breath is a connecting force…it connects the human being with the outside world and the outside world with his inner world. Breathing is an original unceasing movement and therefore actual life" (p. 77).

Yet not all breaths are the same; some are quick, shallow and irregular, others deep, rhythmic, and drawn out. There is the kind of unconscious breathing when we have adapted to our surrounding environment, a type of breath that seems to have forgotten the multitude of scents in the external smellscape. But when we move to a new environment, or a novel or unusual aroma infiltrates our noses, our breathing changes. We may take deeper breaths if the scent is pleasant, as from a restaurant, or we may breathe shallow to avoid an unpleasant aroma such as a gas station bathroom. Yet other times we gasp. Recall that Hillman used the word aisthesis to denote perception and inhalation, but more specifically it means "a breathing in or taking in of the world, the gasp, 'aha,' the 'uh' of the breath in wonder, shock, amazement, an aesthetic response to the image presented" (Hillman, 2014, pp. 39-40). He is referring to a particular kind of breathing experience, something different than a "commonplace inhale." Whether the cause of the gasp is pleasant or unpleasant is less important, only that our breathing has been temporarily arrested. Hillman (2014) again: "What is it to 'take in' or breathe in the world? First, it means aspiring and inspiring the literal presentation of things by gasping…Second, 'taking in' means taking to heart, interiorizing, becoming intimate with" (p. 40).

Once when I was wandering through an alley in Shanghai, China I caught a whiff of something and immediately gasped and almost vomited. I plugged my nose and retreated as fast as I could. Later I reflected on what provoked my gasp and decided it was the scent of cooked meat—rat was my guess. That was not an odor I was expecting to become intimate with, but nevertheless it penetrated my nostrils and I took it to heart as I realized the obvious necessity or preference of some Chinese to eat such an animal. I must acknowledge and point out that because I did not know for certain the source of the stench, my disgust was partially based upon what I imagined the odor to be. "We reach toward beauty and recoil from ugliness as from bodily harm. A mere glance, a line, a little melody starts us up; we catch our breath while ugliness makes us retreat" (Hillman, 2016e, pp. 327-328).

Disgusting and ugly scents can cause us to gasp as instinctually as does a delicious and beautiful aroma. When it comes to scent-evoked memories, a gasp is often experienced when a scent arrives unexpectedly and we are taken by surprise. Ekman (2003) offers his view on the experience of surprise:

> Surprise is the briefest of all the emotions, lasting only a few seconds at most. In a moment surprise passes as we figure out what is happening, and then surprise merges into fear, amusement, relief, anger, disgust, and so forth, depending upon what it was that surprised us, or it may be followed by

no emotion at all if we determine that the
surprising event was of no consequence. (p. 148)
Whether surprise is actually an emotion or not is
debatable, but the point is that the duration of surprise is
short, other emotions are usually involved, and a gasp
usually accompanies the experience of surprise. Casey
puts it like this: "The sudden salience…surprise means
'take on,' 'take upon.' It grabs me in that way…not as
meaning—that's something later, that's something else.
This is the moment of surprise" (as cited in Hillman,
2016b, p. 412). Casey's definition of surprise, to "take on"
or "take upon" is strikingly similar to aisthesis, which we
learned means "a breathing in or taking in of the world."
To inhale a scent that surprisingly evokes a vivid and
affectively charged memory can create a feeling of wonder
and awe regardless of the content of the memory; it can
sometimes be quite jarring, such as my experience in
Brazil.

Yet surprise is different than a shock or a startle;
the physical and somatic reactions need to be
differentiated. According to Ekman (2003), the expression
on our face when we are startled is the exact opposite of a
surprise expression. When we are surprised our eyes open
wide, eyebrows are raised, and our jaw drops open. In
shock or startle our eyes close tight, eyebrows lower, and
our lips press together (p. 151). I do not know about our
breath, but I suspect that during shock we hold our breath
while surprise leads to a gasp. I am making this distinction
because what I have been proposing with the gasping of
certain scents has, I believe, more to do with surprise than
shock. I have not come across any research that

demonstrates scents to actually provoke a true shock response.

I would like to return once again to my experience in Brazil. Recall that when I inhaled the scent of the unknown woman I gasped in surprise, for she smelled exactly like my former girlfriend. This recognition released a multitude of memories from my previous relationship. As Ekman pointed out, surprise is usually followed by other emotions. In my case, the emotions and feelings that followed my initial surprise were sadness, nostalgia, arousal, dismay, and awe. What could account for such powerful emotions? Here is one researcher's perspective: "The implicit nature of olfactory representations and the low frequency of autobiographical memories probably underlie the experienced 'suddenness' of an odor-evoked memory that may bias the notion of its powerfulness" (Larsson, Willander, Karlsson, & Arshamian, 2014, p. 3). "Implicit nature of olfactory representations" I take to mean unconscious (memory) images within the psyche. Larsson seems to saying that the reason odor-evoked biographical memories can seem so powerful is because they are unconscious and therefore arise "suddenly," and also because of their rarity. Whether the powerfulness is biased or not seems less important to the fact that it occurred.

Is not the reason we gasp in surprise due to the nature of awe itself? We experience wonder and awe precisely because something is rare and also that we are overwhelmed by something incomprehensible (Ekman, 2003, pp. 194-195). The somatic response of our bodies is the first indication of wonder and awe. We get goose bumps; tingling in shoulders and back of neck, change in respiration (deep inhalations and exhalations, sighs), shaking of the head in incredulity. Further, "when we feel wonder, we stand still, we are not impelled to action" (Ekman, 2003, p. 195). Even when we breathe there are two brief still points—at the end of the exhalation before we inhale again, and at the apex of our inhalation, just before we exhale. However, when we gasp, the pause seems to last a little longer.

The standing still in awe and wonder reminds me of Joseph Campbell's (1986) writing on James Joyce's *Portrait of the Artist as a Young Man*, where the protagonist, Stephen, speaks of proper and improper art. "We speak of esthetic arrest," writes Campbell. "One is not moved to physical action of any kind, but held in a sensational (esthetic) contemplation and enjoyment" (p. 93). With aromas we tend to move toward a pleasant smell and away from scents we find offensive or disgusting. But in those rare moments when we gasp from a surprising scent that triggers an emotional memory image, we stop and become still, temporarily arrested in a state of awe. "In that awe-full image of stopping there is a rush of wings, an animal power in the insubstantial air" (Berry, 2008, p. 148).

Whether we sniff or gasp, our breath carries scent molecules from the world into us and then we exhale them back into the world. In that short time span our bodies and psyches may be so affected that time and distance can evaporate and we are left shaking our heads in wonder at how something as invisible and intangible as an aroma could assault us in such a way. There is something beautiful and healthy in the simplicity of that brief experience. I say beautiful because of the intimate and sometimes emotional relationship between self, aroma, and world. The experience is healthy for both our body and psyche because of the way in which we expand our diaphragm a little more than usual, as well as for the surprise and awe which takes us out of our habitual mode of being. As Rilke (2011) wrote, "nothing can move you if you do not allow for it to surprise you with an unimaginable beauty. Beauty is always something we come to, but we don't know what this something is" (p. 123). It is as if we need scents to awaken us, to occasionally arouse us from a slumber so as to remember the beauty of our lives. Perhaps we need to gasp in surprise and confront our own particular scent images, the ones that have stayed with us, haunted us, and the beautiful ones that have helped us dream. Like Bachelard (1960/1969) writes, "great dreamers thus know how to breathe the past" (pp. 136-137).

Beauty, Aesthetics, and Context

Sweet in her green dell
the flower of beauty slumbers,
Lulled by the faint breezes
sighing through her hair;
Sleeps she and hears not
the melancholy numbers
Breathed to my sad lute 'mid the lonely air.
~George Darley, *"Love Song"*

*Beauty is an instance which plainly shows that
culture is not simply utilitarian in its aims,
for the lack of beauty is a thing
we cannot tolerate in civilization.*
~Sigmund Freud, *Civilization and It's Discontents*

*Under heaven all can see beauty as beauty
only because there is ugliness*
–Lao Tsu, *Tao Te Ching, "Two,"*

In 1930, Sigmund Freud wrote:
Happiness in life is sought first and foremost in the
enjoyment of beauty, wherever it is to be found by
our senses. The enjoyment of beauty produces a
particular, mildly intoxicating kind of sensation.
There is no very evident use in beauty; the
necessity of it for cultural purposes is not apparent,
and yet civilization could not do without it.
(1930/2010, pp. 38-39)
With this observation Freud was not just pointing out that
happiness and beauty are related, or that experiencing
beauty simply feels good, but that it is fundamental to our
being. Joseph Campbell (1986) would agree: "Beauty is
thus a value, a good, an end in itself. Ugliness depresses,
beauty exhilarates, heightening the sense of life, which
again is a good in itself" (p. 92). We do not know what
Freud and Campbell mean exactly by "beauty," but it is
likely they would have said beauty includes great works of
art like paintings or sculptures or something visual in
nature like flowers. Perhaps because our eyes are our

dominant sense organs we tend to speak about beauty as something visual.

But beauty is more than what the eyes see or even what the ears hear. "Aesthetic experience is thus not limited to the official art world. It can occur in any aspect of our everyday lives—whenever we take note of, or create for ourselves, new coherences that are not part of our conventionalized mode of perception or thought" (Lakoff & Johnson, 1980, p. 236). As a "new coherence" I therefore would like to propose that scents are a form of beauty as well. Moreover, we need beautiful scents in our lives because, "the soul shrivels without images and sensations of beauty" (Hillman, 1999, p. 116). What, then, gives a fragrance its beauty?

The study and philosophy of beauty has traditionally fallen under the subject of aesthetics. The word *aesthetic* comes from the Greek *aisthetikos*: "perceptive"; *aisthanesthai* "to perceive, to feel" (Campbell, 1986, p. 93). The two parts taken together thus have to do with perception (sensory experience), as well as with feeling. The conceptualization of aesthetics therefore has to do with both external sensory stimuli as well as our internal feelings regarding the sensory stimuli. This conceptualization is not solely a cognitive process:

> Conceptual structure is not merely a matter of the intellect—it involves all the natural dimensions of our experience, including aspects of our sense experiences: color, shape, texture, sound, etc. These dimensions structure not only mundane experience but aesthetic experience as well. (Lakoff & Johnson, 1980, p. 235)

Scents too are natural dimensions of our experience that ultimately structure our aesthetic lives. Again, this is more than an intellectual activity, but rather more like a heartfelt response or an animal instinct. "This heart awakens in the aesthetic response. It is an animal awareness to the face of things" (Hillman, 2014, p. 37). When I asked a friend of mine why she loves the smell of wet paint, she said, "I don't know, I just do." "The aesthetic judgment is, as Kant said, independent of logic," says Hillman. "It comes spontaneously, like a movement of the heart, even as that reaction to ugliness: 'I can't stand it. Take it away'…Aesthetics in everyday affairs" (pp. 47-48). We perceive and we feel, and our aesthetic judgments are structured as much through our sense of smell as through our other senses.

Hillman (1972) notes that "the criteria of aesthetics—unity, line, rhythm, tension, elegance—may be transposed to the psyche, giving us a new set of qualities for appreciating what is going on in a psychological process" (p. 101). In order to understand what makes a scent beautiful we need to ground ourselves within the psyche itself, for it is the soul that "mediates the beauty of the invisible inner world to the world of outer forms" (p. 102). This means returning to psychic images and our emotions while paying special attention to the context in which they appear. In this particular case of my research we are investigating the exceptional nature of beautiful scent memories. Herz (2007) summarizes this idea well: "It is not the 'long-forgottenness,' but rather the unique connection between olfaction, emotion, and memory that makes scent-evoked memories so special" (p.

74). We therefore need to look at olfaction, emotion, and memory within a proper context.

Olfactory research often uses the phrase "odor hedonics," which means the degree of pleasure or displeasure from an odor. "The most important aspect of an odor," writes Engen (1982), "has generally been believed to be its hedonic effect" (p. 11). Whether or not an odor's hedonic effect is the most important aspect of an odor is less important than understanding that odor hedonics is a useful conceptual structure to measure or qualify both pleasantness and beauty. In other words, I contend that we can use the hedonic terms "pleasure" and "displeasure" in the same way we use the words "beautiful" and "ugly." Instead of or in addition to asking, "What makes a scent beautiful?", we can ask, "What makes a scent pleasurable?" We are of course back to dualistic terms, so we must not forget that there are subtle variations that exist on a continuum between beautiful/ugly and pleasure/displeasure. But for the sake of simplicity, I will use, like most researchers, binary terms to speak of odor hedonics.

Let us return to the important premise of context. Herz (2007) maintains that, "emotion is a central and fundamental feature of odor perception, odor learning, and odor memory" (p. xiii). She also introduces a key term called "odor-associative learning," the definition of which is: "how you feel when you first encounter a particular scent determines your future hedonic perception of it" (p. 39). In other words, the emotions we feel when encountering a new scent is a significant factor in determining whether that scent will be pleasurable or not in the future. Then, "once an odor association has been acquired, the contribution of the odor is to facilitate retrieval of *the context in which it was experienced*" (Engen, 1991 p. 118). For example, I adore the aroma of clary sage essential oil because the first time I smelled it was at a weekend workshop during an exceptionally joyous time in my life. Put simply, "the emotions associated to an odor will determine how that odor is later perceived and experienced" (Herz, 2007, p. 79).

It is likely that every adult has at least one memory of getting sick from a particular food or drink and thereafter feels disgust or a similar emotion when encountering the smell of the provoking substance. Herz (2007) explains that, "being sick just once after ingesting a certain food causes avoidance of the substance that triggered the illness, and especially its scent, for a long time thereafter" (p. 51).

The most recent example in my life occurred when I ate a bowl of cereal using coconut milk creamer (normally used with coffee) instead of regular milk and got violently sick several hours later. Part of me knew that the creamer was much too thick, rich, and sweet for my stomach to handle, but I used it nevertheless. To this day I cannot drink or smell that creamer or anything resembling it. Even the scent image and somatic memory of it as I write this now makes me a little queasy. Before making me sick coconut creamer had for me a somewhat pleasant, but mostly meaningless neutral aroma. Herz (2007) elucidates: "Although this scent is not inherently good or bad, the context you are in when you first consciously experience it is bad, and therefore this initially meaningless odor acquires the negative valence of your feelings" (p. 38). In the realm of aesthetics, coconut milk creamer for me is now ugly.

The worn-out idiom, "beauty is in the eye of the beholder," reflects our culture's belief that beauty is essentially subjective and personal. (It also illustrates the emphasis we have historically placed on the visual aspect of aesthetics) If we were to transfer this idiom onto scents, we would say something like "pleasure is in the nose of the smeller." According to research in the natural sciences this appears to be true. "Adults across this planet do not agree on what smells good and what smells bad—even for the stench of death. Culture, which conveys another form of learning, explains how and why" (Herz, 2007, p. 35). Cultural learning is contrasted with direct learning of odors through personal experiences with them. I have heard that in parts of India, for instance, dead bodies are cremated outdoors in public view and the locals do not seem to be bothered by the smell. This could be due to personal experience with burning bodies or it may be culturally taught. "What your culture tells you is good or bad becomes incorporated into your perception lexicon, even if you haven't had direct experience with the object in question" (p. 46). I suspect most non-Indians would plug their nose in disgust and flee as quickly as possible if they were exposed to the aroma of burning human bodies. Cultural conditioning certainly plays a role in scent preferences, but to what extent, is difficult to say. Herz does however point out that "it is not until children are about eight years old that they start to show odor preferences that match the responses of the adults in their culture…there is *no* data that infants show predictable—innate—reactions to smells" (p. 33).

Would most Americans, for instance, repel in horror from the smell of grilled chicken in a public park? Not likely, as that is a common and culturally accepted aroma. "Cultural learning can be divisive in eliciting specific emotional responses to fragrances," notes Herz (2007, p. 96). Yet there are wide variations of odor preferences even among people of the same culture (Gilbert, 2008, p. 234). My father, who has been a vegetarian for many years, would groan and plug his nose if he smelled grilled chicken while walking through a park.

The context of where and when an odor is smelled is also significant. Staying with the example above, if the smell of grilled chicken was inhaled in a hospital or day spa it may provoke an adverse reaction. "The relationship between odor and behavior is context determined," explains Engen (1991). "Where an odor is smelled is an important factor. Even body odor and tobacco smoke, which figure prominently in studies of indoor air quality, are not universally disliked, although they are generally considered objectionable" (pp. 10-11). To illustrate the importance of context in determining whether a scent is beautiful or ugly, I will share some memories of body odor, tobacco, and alcohol.

When I was a freshman in high school I started to attend informal school dances. These dances were different than anything I had ever experienced. First, people actually danced, often quite wild and uninhibited. Second, there were girls that were growing into their womanhood. Third, many people arrived to the dance intoxicated with alcohol or drugs. My emotions at the dances were usually a combination of excitement, nervousness, and sensory pleasure. It was the first time that I danced physically close to girls—not slow-dance close, but hip, belly, and neck close—moving fast, something that we called "freaking" or "grinding." When I danced with girls I breathed in their sweaty youth, a sweat of sexual tension, changing hormones, and self-exploration. I could smell alcohol or tobacco on their heated breath, skin, and on their clothes, all of which overpowered whatever perfume they happened to be wearing. I loved all these scents for what they represented to me: new experiences, exploration of our physical bodies, release of tension, and maturation into young adults. Had someone asked me at that time what scent acted as an aphrodisiac, I would have said my high school dances. A comment on aphrodisiacs by Engen (1991) is worth sharing here:

> An odor is only capable of conjuring up the memory of a sensual experience and does not directly motivate such behavior. Any odor that happened to be present on an occasion—the body odor of a partner, her perfume, the diesel odor of his car—may act like an aphrodisiac or a repellent, depending on the nature of the encounter. (p. 120)

In a different context the smell of alcohol on a person's breath was typically unpleasant for me. Most human sweat I disliked in any context, especially male sweat, and the scent of cigarettes I always despised. But at my high school dances the scents were, to me, exquisitely beautiful. Looking back, it was the entire smellscape that captivated me. An assortment of female sweat, my own sweat, even the sweat of other guys, plus lingering alcohol, pot, tobacco, and perfume combined to create an atmosphere of youthful excitement for me.

Years later I would experience similar aromas in adult nightclubs, but I didn't care for the smells anymore. The scents of women, sweat, alcohol, pot, and tobacco—all were there, but they didn't evoke the same feelings that I had at my high school dances. In these situations, I was more self-conscious and less confident. Men were on the competitive prowl, woman were less friendly, more cautious and defensive. I can recall holding my breath in negative anticipation before I entered clubs. In fact, most of my nightclub experiences were unpleasant and therefore the scents are ugly and evoke disgust when I recall those memories. Herz (2007) reminds us that "our expectations and the situational context we are in can also drastically influence what we construe an odor to be and therefore what hedonic properties we assign it" (p. 55). Thus, not only do our emotions and the contextual environment influence our perception of a beautiful scent, but also our expectations.

We began this section with the premise that beauty is fundamental to our lives and that aromas are a type of beauty that can be judged aesthetically. We also learned that the context in which we experience odors is an important factor in determining our hedonic or aesthetic perceptions of those scents. "Odor perception is situational, contextual, and ecological," writes Engen (1991, p. 86). The context contains all aspects of our phenomenological scent experience: the place and situation, who was there, what was happening, how we felt, input from our other senses, and our personal and cultural expectations. If context contains all these aspects, it is the associations between them that create the inner smellscape and ultimately lead us to call a scent memory beautiful or ugly. Engen reminds us that, "odors are not stored in memory as unique entities. Rather, they are always interrelated with other sensory perceptions—gustatory, cutaneous, visual, auditory, and thermal—that happen to coincide with them" (p. 87). In fact, this appears to be the case for all of our other senses. Sights, sounds, tastes, and tactile sensations are likewise not stored in memory as unique entities. Let us recall the notion of synesthesia from the previous chapter. We learned that our fundamental, pre-conceptual experience is inherently synesthetic; sensory modalities are not separate, but intertwine, intercommunicate, and overlap to form a unitary whole (Abram, 1996, pp. 60-61).

However, not all our scent memories are clear and traceable to their origins. As we discovered earlier, associations are often formed automatically and unconsciously. Herz (2007) explains:

> Intrinsic to the fact that we form associations to odors that determine our hedonic responses to them is that an association is a type of memory. An association can be vague and you many only *feel* that a certain smell is good for bad, with no specific recollection in mind, but it can also bring forth complex and intense personal memories. (p. 60)

Regardless of whether we can remember exactly how and when a scent memory was formed, our aesthetic reaction and animal reflex to a particular scent betrays our aesthetic judgment. "One's heart is waked, not by the form of the work, but by its content" (Campbell, 1986, p. 96). We are moved not by the smell itself, which is the "form," but by its "content," which are the associations of all the elements within a particular context. Ultimately, we must be moved and our heart must awaken because, as Freud said, happiness in life is sought first and foremost in the enjoyment of beauty, wherever it is to be found by our senses, so that "beauty apprehended should have this power to illuminate the senses, still the mind, and enchant the heart" (as cited in Campbell, 1986, p. 101). What, then, are the beautiful scent memories that enchant our hearts?

Memories of Beauty

Blossoms will run away
Cakes reign but a Day,
But Memory like Melody
Is pink Eternally
~Emily Dickinson, *1883*

For centuries your fragrance has called
its sweetest names across to us;
suddenly it floats in the air like fame.
Still, we can't find the word, we grope ...
And memory betrays us, goes over with all
we've begged from the responding hours.
~R. M. Rilke

I saw how all the trembling ages past,
Moulded to her by deep and deeper breath,
Neared to the hour when
Beauty breathes her last
And knows herself in death.
~A.E., "The Great Breath"

As we have discovered thus far, beautiful scent memories that enchant our hearts cannot be generalized; they are particular and specific to each person. Even when people agree that common scents evoke deep pleasure (such as freshly cut grass or oranges, for instance), the scent memory will be full of idiosyncratic associations, images, and somatic sensations. Moreover, these memories can be aroused in more than one way.

There are at least three different triggers for scent memories: the first happens through direct inhalation of the source odor. The second occurs when a non-olfactory sense (sight, sound, touch), by association, sparks a memory. The third way a memory is retrieved is through our imagination without the actual fragrance present. The first trigger has generally been given the most attention from the natural sciences and is often referred to as odor-evoked autobiographical memory. In the second case semantics typically dominate the research, which tends to use written or oral verbal stimuli as cues to test scent recall. Finally, recalling scent memories without any stimuli, using only our imagination, is less researched and is scientifically more ambiguous.

Therefore, to do memory justice I must give attention to each of these ways that bring forth beautiful scent memories. The telling of scent stories will help us accomplish this task. Not only do stories provide concrete examples, they also reflect our deepest values. As Hillman (1972) writes:

> What we hold close in our imaginal world are not just images and ideas but living bits of soul; when they are spoken, a bit of soul is carried with them. When we tell our tales, we give away our souls. (p. 182)

I will now share living bits of my soul with one such tale. A few weeks ago, I was walking through a fruit orchard close to my house and came upon a plum tree. There were several ripe, dark purple plums lying on the ground so I picked one up. It felt warm from having soaked in the sun. I gave it a quick look-over and a few sniffs, and then tossed it in my mouth. As soon as I broke it open Summer exploded throughout my entire body and psyche. It wasn't the memory of any particular summer but of all the summers of my youth. Bachelard (1960/1969) explains:

> The pure memory has no date. It has a *season*. The season is the fundamental mark of memories. What sun or what wind was there that memorable day? That is the question which gives the right tension of reminiscence. Then the memories become great images, magnified, magnifying images. (p. 116)

One small plum contained for me the entire season of summer—a grand image indeed. The smell and taste left me with a felt sense of warm joy and giddy happiness as my eyes widened in pleasure. I moaned as the sweet and juicy flesh and astringent skin evoked memories of long warm days and cool nights, and hours at the beach, pool, and park with my family and friends. Images rushed forth of sitting on sand and grass eating fresh fruit whose juice dripped down my face, and sticky hands that I rinsed with garden hoses or ocean water. Keller (2009) certainly would have related to my experience: "The odor of fruits wafts me to my Southern home, to my childish frolics in the peach orchard. Other odors, instantaneous and fleeting, cause my heart to dilate joyously or contract with remembered grief" (pp. 26-27).

As I greedily popped another plum in my mouth I recalled that my childhood home had a pluot tree on the side of our house where I would pick fruit off the ground or pluck from the tree. (A pluot is a plum-apricot hybrid). There is a difference eating seasonal fruit off the tree versus fruit in the supermarket that is out of season. I ate apples, bananas, and oranges year-round. But plums, pluots, apricots, white peaches, and nectarines I only ate (and still do) in summer. Had I come across a peach or apricot tree instead of the plum, the warm ripe fruit would have probably evoked the memory of summer in similar fashion, as the associations between those fruits and summer were just as strong. As Herz (2007) points out, "intrinsic to the fact that we form associations to odors that determine our hedonic responses to them is that an association is a type of memory" (p. 60).

Since taste is primarily the result of olfactory stimulation (Gilbert, 2008, pp. 91-94), we can say that when I ate the plum I experienced an odor-evoked autobiographical memory, a direct provocation of memory caused by the source odor and taste. According to recent research, there is a physiological reason for this that is quite ancient. "Memories triggered by the sense of smell rely on the integrity of the limbic system and are typically old, more vivid, often emotional, and relatively rare as compared to autobiographical information evoked by our primary sensory systems" (Larsson et al., 2014, p. 2). Since our limbic system is one of the parts of our body we share with many mammals and reptiles, it makes me wonder if it is partially responsible for our instinctual aesthetic reactions, our immediate response to a beautiful or ugly scent association.

I think what makes the fruit-scent memory beautiful for me is that it captures an entire season— summer—which is my favorite, when I most come alive and thrive. Summer revives me and therefore smelling or eating seasonal fruit off the ground or tree, like plums, is an internal vivification. Bachelard (1960/1969) speaks to this enlivening:

> How can we avoid speaking of psychological beauty when confronted with an attractive event from our inner life? This beauty is within us, at the bottom of memory. It is the beauty of a flight which revives us, which puts the dynamism of one of life's beauties within us. (p. 101)

It is as if the fresh plum awakened decades of summers which had laid dormant within me, and which held the beauty of my life throughout all the seasonal changes. Ackerman (1990) offers this perspective: "Smells detonate softly in our memory like poignant land mines, hidden under the weedy mass of many years and experiences. Hit a tripwire of smell, and memories explode all at once. A complex vision leaps out of the undergrowth" (p. 5). I'd like to think that the plum was just waiting for me to taste and smell its sweetness so that my heart could once again be enchanted.

Thirteenth century Catholic saint Albertus Magnus called the power of some memories *metaphorica*, and wrote that, "the wonderful moves the memory more than the ordinary" (as cited in Hillman, 1972, p. 180). Although the next scent memory I will share was not provoked by a direct scent, I was reminded of a past experience that was, for a young American guy, anything but ordinary. As a colleague of mine was telling me about his recent trip to Japan I was suddenly seized by the scent of leeks and wet soil.

Ten years ago a Japanese friend of mine invited me to visit her family in Japan. Part of my time there was spent helping her parents pull leeks from the deep rich earth and then stack, bundle, and deliver them to a packaging factory. Despite the hard physical work, I thoroughly enjoyed the whole experience. To be in an open field with nothing but rows of leeks, inhaling damp soil and pungent-sweet leeks, below thick winter clouds, hearing nothing but Japanese words and crow cries—I felt like I was living in a movie a hundred years ago. For lunch we would sit on the ground and eat hot noodle soup and drink green tea. I recall feeling intensely grateful for such a simple and authentic experience that few tourists would ever have. The air seemed to pulse with clean, sharp, and ancient scent molecules that penetrated deep inside my lungs. I wondered how many others had toiled in those same fields and if they noticed all the aromas as I had.

I can't recall all the details of my farming experience, but rather a few striking images and an overall feeling of joy. As Cowan (2002) wisely points out, "what memory retains is the mood, the emotion, the subjective perception and experience of a reality—the psychic lens twisted in a particular way—but not always the completely accurate reproduction of a literal event" (p. 58). I don't think my soul is interested in literal and accurate long-term memories anyway. Rather, I believe it wants memories of beauty, however those memories are formed.

Moreover, it doesn't take long for a beautiful memory to make its mark on the soul. As Engen (1991) points out, "a long-term odor memory can be established with only one exposure. An episode is tagged in memory with whatever odor happens to be present. And then, like a bad habit, this odor connection is difficult to unlearn and forget" (p. 6). More recent research supports Engen's findings: "The first olfactory associations enjoy a privileged brain representation that is underlined by the hippocampus" (Saive et al., 2014, p. 6). Just listening to a colleague speak about Japan sparked the scent image of leeks from years ago. It was almost as if the spoken words were a symbol, a partial stand-in for the actual odor. Perhaps Sperber (1975) is correct when we say that "symbolism thus provides a second mode of access to memory: evocation, appropriate when invocation fails" (p. 121). Here is an instance where the actual scent was not needed to evoke a scent memory; simply hearing certain words were sufficient.

To recall a scent memory without the presence of an actual fragrance can be difficult for many people. Moreover, this is a challenging subject to write about because olfactory research does not agree on the process of imaginative odor recall. Researchers also question whether it is actually possible to conjure an odor sensation from memory at all. This topic will be taken up more thoroughly at the end of this chapter. For now, let us look at some of these ideas on odor memories and the imagination.

On one hand, we can affirm that, "the strong anatomical connection between olfactory and memory structures makes olfaction a privileged sense for accessing memories" (Saive et al., 2014, p. 2). These researchers are, I believe, referring to memory accessed by actual scent inhalation. On the other hand, observe Gilbert's (2008) take on scent memory without an odor present: "To re-experience the smells of times gone by, one needs the *actual stuff,* without it, written references and therefore literature eventually lose their power" (p. 206). According to Engen (1991), a different psychological process may be taking place when the source odor is absent:

> Most people believe that they can indeed recall odors, but they will usually agree after further introspection that what comes to mind is some object associated with an odor, such as the visual image of a lemon rather than a lemony odor. These related images do not bring with them the sensation of odor, and therefore they entail a different mental state than that elicited by the actual odors. (p. 6)

While I do not doubt Engen's observation that a "different mental state" is taking place, I wonder whether we could, with practice, experience the actual odor image as a physiological sensation. But even if physical sensations are not possible, I propose that if it is necessary to bring a "lemony odor" to mind by imagining an optical image of a lemon. In fact, it would seem that all the other objects that are associated with the scent memory should be gathered and included to create a rich inner smellscape. Herz (2007) offers her perspective on this matter:

> I believe the reason why we are so poor at imagining odors compared to other sensations is because we do not need abstract odors to survive. We use smell to tell us what to approach and what to avoid when we come across an item in question—*this food is good and this one is bad.* We don't use odors to construct maps or abstract schemas of our world. (p. 88)

To differentiate odor memory via the imagination versus recalling memories via concrete scent is a challenging task. Several questions need to be asked: which part of the psyche or body is capable of what? For instance, the limbic system may do one thing while the psyche does something else. How to measure such differences? If there is too much overlap between physiology and the imagination, can we even proceed with this line of inquiry? Further research is clearly needed. But let us return to Herz's (2007) assertion that we do not need abstract odors to survive. I would like to add that even if we don't need abstract odors to survive physically, our souls need beautiful scent images for its survival. "The soul shrivels without images and sensations of beauty," wrote Hillman (1999, p. 116). How, then, do we recollect beautiful scent memories that animate us?

As I have noted throughout my research, strong emotions felt in the body are crucial and essential components to the formation of scent associations. For example, "mommy scent is soothing because the emotions associated with Mama become attached to her scent" (Herz, 2007, p. 154). Even when we can't recall how or when an association to an aroma was formed, our emotions embedded within the scent are an indication of its importance:

> We may have only a vague, fleeting memory of the literal circumstances of a long-past event, but the emotions attached to that wisp of memory are still sharp, piercing, lodged permanently and precisely in the imagination and in the body. (Cowan, 2002, pp. 63-64)

Thus, to imagine scent memories we must be in our bodies (not stuck in our intellect), we must attune ourselves to our vibrating soma, and be able and willing to feel strong emotions. "The capacity to feel deeply," writes Cowan, "is in part dependent on the ability to remember images of deeply felt experience" (p. 57).

As an example, I will share a scent memory that called up solely through my imagination. I spent eight years of my childhood and teenage years in the Boy Scouts. During these years I averaged about six camping trips per year. Some of these trips were in the Sierra Mountains of central and northern California. I can recall the first time I discovered a particular Pine tree whose fragrance almost made me faint with pleasure. After setting up our tents a small group of us set out to gather firewood. To the side of a trail a sweet aroma caught my attention. I moved in the direction of a large tree with thick bark. When I was about five feet from it I gasped, as the tree emitted a delicious butterscotch-like aroma. I got closer to the tree and stuck my nose within a space between the bark and inhaled what seemed to me was waffles with maple syrup. How could such a tree produce such a yummy fragrance, I did not know, nor care. I only thought and felt, "Oh! I love this forest and everything in it, especially these trees." It turns out the type of trees are called Ponderosa or Jeffery Pines. To smell those trees made my body come alive with vigorous and youthful energy. I yelled to my friends to come smell these incredible trees. We all put our noses against the sappy bark and enjoyed the strong aromas, often described as vanilla, cinnamon, coconut, or lemon cookies. Despite being at high elevation, which apparently decreases our olfactory function (Altundag, Salihoglu, Cayonu, Cingi, Tekeli, et al., 2014, pp. 615-618) the fragrance was bold, thick, and intoxicating to us.

Those early experiences camping in the Sierras were a time of exploration, of bonding with other boys and men, and immersion in nature. I pondered how few of my friends back home would ever get to smell these wild trees, untouched by chainsaws and telephone wires. Though some may doubt, as I write this I am easily recalling the odor of those sticky sweet pines. I am also hearing the crunch of pine needles and leaves below my feet, and I can see the sun beams through the trees land upon the pines, warming their thick bark, which so generously offers to me their enticing fragrance. My senses are all stimulated, my breath is deep, and my heart is full of beauty. Although it has been many years since I last inhaled a Jeffrey or Ponderosa Pine, if I were to be blindfolded in a forest I could identify those trees in an instant. Keller (2009) would understand what I mean:

> The dear odors of those I love are so definite, so unmistakable, that nothing can quite obliterate them. If many years should elapse before I saw an intimate friend again, I think I should recognize his

odor instantly in the heart of Africa, as promptly as
would my brother that barks. (p. 30)
That a beautiful scent memory cannot be easily obliterated
is testimony to the lasting power of meaningful images. A
beautiful image must also be accessible to recall in some
way or another. As Bachelard (1943/1988) writes:

> As long as an image does not reveal its value by
> beauty, or, to speak more dynamically, feeling the
> value of beauty…or find a place for one who
> imagines in a world of beauty, then it is not
> fulfilling its dynamic function. (p. 261)

In other words, an image must move us—arouse, provoke,
stir, perturb, or arrest us in some way. As I have shown,
memories of beauty do this to us. But so do ugly and
disgusting memories. "All experience goes to show that
beauty needs her opposite as a condition of her existence"
(Jung, 1923/1971, p. 85). The unpleasant and grotesque
need our attention too, for these images are also part of
our soul.

Memories of Disgust

There are many graves and corpses in us,
an evil stench of decomposition.
~C.G. Jung, *Liber Novus*

It's dark and the stench of manure is strong
but all that vanishes when friendship enters
~Rumi, *The Essential Rumi*

> *Yet in the watchful, warm animal*
> *is the weight and care of deep sadness.*
> *For what so often overwhelms us*
> *adheres in the animal as well—a memory...*
> ~R. M. Rilke, *"The Eight Elegy"*

We have spent much of this chapter occupied with beauty, and rightly so, for it is fundamental to our lives, a guiding force which adds texture and vitality to our experiences. Yet we must now turn in a different direction, one that is equally important though not as popular in our culture today: the Ugly. The path that will get us there is depth psychology, which, "has always worked with its eye attentive to the ugly" (Hillman, 2014, p. 46). We therefore have the opportunity to engage more fully with the world and ourselves when we face the disgusting, dark, and ugly scent memories that have unequivocally left their mark.

"The relation to ugliness guides our self-knowledge," writes Hillman (2014). "Ugliness is the guide because aesthetic responses occur most strongly in relation with the ugly. Plutinus says: Sensations of the ugly and evil impress us more violently than those of what is agreeable" (p. 47). It seems unnecessary to me to debate whether pleasant or unpleasant scents move us more strongly or which ones impress us more deeply. I am not interested in the following kind of research either: "Odor-evoked memories of aversive events were more detailed than memories evoked by auditory but not visual cues" (Larsson et al., 2014, p 3). What is important, however, is that beautiful and ugly scent memories exist at all, and that they stay with us for many years. The task then is to give voice to how these striking images manifest in their own particular way. As a first example, let us look at a scene in a novel by Émile Zola (2000).

> When Gervaise turned into the entry of the Hotel Boncoeur, her tears again mastered her. It was a dark, narrow passage, with a gutter for the dirty water running alongside the wall; and the stench which she again encountered there caused her to think of the fortnight she had passed in the place with Lantier — a fortnight of misery and quarrels, the recollection of which was now a bitter regret. It seemed to bring her abandonment home to her. (p. 32)

We can see how the odor of dirty water in a gutter evoked intense memories of sadness and misery. The smell further contributed to more complex thoughts and feelings such as regret and abandonment. Had the character Gervaise had a joyous past experience with the man Lantier, the hotel through which she walked, despite the gutter water, would have given her a different feeling. This is because, as Engen (1991) notes, "the sense of smell is very sensitive, learns quickly, and does not forget, but it is not very discriminating and it has no judgment about what is important to remember and what is best forgotten" (p. 8). Unfortunately for Gervaise, the hotel entrance now had an ugly association, to which she apparently could do nothing to change.

As with beauty, there are degrees of intensity when we experience disgust and ugliness. "Odor-evoked memories can also elicit unpleasant emotions. Indeed, they can be exceptionally potent triggers in post-traumatic stress disorder (PTSD)…depending upon an individual's past experience with an odor, the emotional states and responses that it elicits can be very negative" (Herz, 2016, p. 4). A patient of mine recently got back from four years of military service in Afghanistan. He mentioned to me how difficult it is for him in the summer because the bar-b-q aromas of cooked meat sometimes trigger terrible memories of burned bodies. In his case the feeling of disgust is not easy to unlearn. Ekman (2003) defines disgust as "a feeling of aversion…a smell that you want to block out of your nasal passage or move away from calls forth disgust. Even the thought of how something repulsive might smell brings out strong disgust" (pp. 172-173).

When I was a young child I was given a pink antibiotic liquid when I had an ear infection. It didn't taste too bad, something like artificial bubblegum or cherry, but because I took it only when I had an unpleasant ear infection, the taste and smell later caused me to feel nauseous. Engen (1991) explains.

> Having first learned one association to an odor, it is difficult for us to replace the association with another one. Odor memory fits the saying about teaching old dog new tricks. This is why, for example, it is difficult to get over aversions to food flavors. (p. 7)

Over the years whenever I encounter any scent or flavor resembling that pink medicine, I always get a little queasy.

A simple way to tell if a scent is disgusting, according to Ekman (2003), is to "pay attention to the feelings in your throat, the beginning of a slight gagging. The sensations in your upper lip and nostrils are increased" (p. 183). Other physical reactions to the feeling of disgust include nose wrinkling and a raised upper lip (p.

184). Just as we may gasp and open our eyes wide when we encounter a surprisingly pleasant scent, so too our face, throat, and stomach present their own response to ugly and revolting aromas. Sometimes all it takes is a single scent to cause such a revolt. At other times we inhale a potpourri of odors. Observe, for instance, this disgusting smellscape portrayed by D. H. Lawrence (1977):

> The air was too scented, it gave no breath. All the lush green-stuff seemed to be issuing its sap, till the air was deathly, sickly with the smell of greenness. There was the perfume of clover, like pure honey and bees. Then there grew a faint acrid tang-they were near the beeches; and then a queer clattering noise, and a suffocating, hideous smell; they were passing a flock of sheep. (p. 51)

In this passage it was not one smell only, but a combination of scents that formed a stifling and horrid kind of feeling. It seems probable that there would be an accompanying feeling of nausea as well. "Certainly, when disgust is intense, there is no question that the sensations are unpleasant, leading to nausea," writes Ekman (2003, p. 182).

Let us recap: sheep, pink antibiotic medicine, cooked meat, and gutter water all lead to the feeling of disgust, but for different reasons. Scents are not inherently pleasant or disgusting; feelings toward specific scents are strongly influenced by their associations and context. Thus the context in which a scent is first experienced is an essential factor in determining whether a scent ushers in the feeling of disgust. Yet, what is the deeper implication of our experience with disgusting scent images?

Hillman (1975) insists that, "if the soul is to be truly moved, a tortured psychology is necessary" (p. 92). I take a tortured psychology to mean any aspect of our psyche that experiences pain, sickness, loathing, loss, betrayal, horror, revulsion, or death. This torture could occur through our own body, the witnessing of others' pain, a dream, or a fantasy image in the present or a memory of the past. As an example of this profound human experience I will share a scent memory that I have never written about, for it is one of the most difficult for me to relive.

Twelve years ago, at the age of 24, I received a phone call the morning after Halloween from my cousin. She asked me if I could check in on her brother, whom the family had not heard from in over two weeks. Her brother (my cousin) was living in an apartment close to the University. I arrived at his second-floor apartment around noon. It was bright and sunny for a day in early November, but the air felt thick and heavy. After knocking on the door and getting no response I tried to open the door but found it locked. So, I walked around to the side and located his bedroom window. The blinds were drawn down but the window was cracked open a few inches. My heart was already beating hard when I noticed two flies buzzing between the glass and blinds. Without hesitating I leaned my face close to the open part of the window, pressed my nose as far forward as possible, and took a few quick sniffs. I flinched backward as the smell from the bedroom confirmed what my intuition and heart had already sensed. He was dead.

I had of course smelled dead animals and insects before, but what I encountered was a little different. There was that typical scent of rottenness, something like old mozzarella cheese, but not as strong. The aroma also had traces of ammonia and honey, a blend of putrid and sweet. Apparently, there are six stages of postmortem decay, each with their own particular odor (Gilbert, 2008, p. 123). I think when I found him his body was at stage five, "dry decay," which begins about a week after death. Some report this stage to smell like "wet fur and old leather" (p. 123). According to the autopsy report I read he had been dead over one week.

My cousin was the kind of guy who always smelled fresh; he showered often and wore high quality cologne. So, it was strange for me to inhale the scent of death from his bedroom. But I knew that what I smelled wasn't he, but his shell; he was gone. Hundreds of memories together from our childhood and adolescence came rushing forward. "That's it," I thought. "No more experiences together in this lifetime." Now all I have left are memories. I stood motionless for a moment and began to feel various emotions move through my body. I don't think it was the smell itself that stirred my emotions, but the memory images of him and our life together that carried the most thrust. Hillman (1999) writes that, "we are moved most strongly by images of dead friends, dead loves, dead family, images that remain poignantly vital even if, or because, they are dead" (p. 101). Yes, my memory images did indeed seem very much alive and vital then, despite the scent of decay still permeating through his bedroom window.

A few moments later I noticed that my heart had stopped pounding, my whole body had relaxed and strangely felt at peace. I looked at the clear sky and had this odd feeling that he was watching me, and that I was the one he wanted to discover his dead body. We were the closest of cousins and he knew I, of all people, was strong enough to handle such an experience. I never actually saw his body, but the confirmation of his physical death, (which I believe his spirit needed) I accomplished through olfaction. "I don't see you, cuz, I smell you. You're dead and it's ok," I tell him.

Fortunately the smell did not linger in my nose, because I needed to take several deep breaths before descending the stairs to inform the apartment manager of what I had found. It is common to feel loathing, abhorrence, and repugnance upon inhaling the stench of death. Ekman (2003) describes the feeling of disgust:

> It's not so much trying to move away as it is getting rid of the offensive object. For example, people may turn away if the offensive object is visual; they may gag or even vomit if it is gustatory or olfactory. (p. 61)

Although I admit the actual odor was unpleasant and caused me to recoil from the bedroom window, as I descended the stairs I actually felt a sense of pride. It was a feeling of strength, of having discovered something terrible with a foul odor but still able to stand and walk without collapsing. Or maybe I was proud simply because I was the first to find him dead, that I would be the one to begin a long chain of phone calls, visits, and ceremonies. Perhaps all of this made the scent of death a little more tolerable.

I did, however, have the benefit of being outside; had I been trapped inside the apartment with the smell, I might have felt stronger disgust and a need to flee. I do not think I will ever "unlearn" the smell of my dead cousin. The memory is too intense, the smell too sharp and unmistakable, as anyone who has ever smelled a dead body would affirm.

> A prototypical odor memory thus originates with a novel experience (though not necessarily a novel odor) and lasts for a lifetime. We all have such individual odor memories that stand out because of the timeless and vivid way in which they bring back the totality of the experience. (Engen, 1991, p. 77)

In a strange way the odor of his dead body is nostalgic for me. I suppose it's because the odor is the last sensory impression I have from his physical being. Maybe the scent memory is serving multiple functions—keeping images of him alive, reminding me of death, and perhaps urging me forward in my own life. "The pathologized image held solemnly is what moves the soul. One dwells upon the affliction or dwells with it, in bed with the leper, in its embrace" (Hillman, 1975, p. 93).

This dwelling of the ugly and grotesque image, the reverent holding of a scent memory, is worked upon and polished in and by our imagination.

> For the soul to be struck to its imaginal depths so that it can gain some intelligence of itself…pathologizing fantasies are required. A bloodied or obscene image in a dream, a hypochondriacal fantasy, a psychosomatic symptom, is a statement in imaginal language that the psyche is being profoundly stirred, and these pathologized fantasies are precisely the focal point

of action and movement in the soul. (Hillman, 1975, p. 92)
Not just images of pathology and disgust, but all of our beautiful and disgusting scent images have the potential to stir us. "The aesthetic, too, opens into the underworld" (Hillman, 1979a, p. 143). In the end we cannot escape our psyche's need to imagine, to form and deform images, and to dig meandering tunnels throughout the deep caverns of our scent memories.

Memory and Imagination

We dream while remembering.
We remember while dreaming.
~Gaston Bachelard, *Poetics of Reverie*

The vapour of old love
Will transfigure through a veil of clarity
~Katatonia, *"Old Heart Falls"*

Spring vanishes the scraps of winter, why
Should there be a question of returning or
Of death in memory's dream? Is spring a sleep?
~Wallace Stevens, *"It Must Change"*

To conclude this chapter on scent memories we must turn to that third factor, the unceasing, intermediary part of our psyche that colors and informs all of our psychic experiences—our imagination. Although a scent can bring the totality of a past experience rapidly back into our consciousness, we still must acknowledge the role played by our imagination. "The imagination ceaselessly revives and illustrates the memory" (Bachelard, 1960/1969, p. 20). We must be willing to accept the possibility that we can truly imagine an odor, to conjure a scent from memory in the same way we can a sight, sound, emotion, or tactile experience. We must put full faith in the workings of our imagination. This is not a difficult task for depth psychology, which grounds itself in the reality of the psyche and gives images and imagination primary value. The natural sciences, however, have more trouble with understanding those parts of our experience that do not fall under their objective methods of investigation; solely subjective or "imaginative" activities often elude objectivity. Herz (2007) puts the problem like this:

> How do you study the ability to remember odors? This is a problem because of another central question in the psychology of smell: can we recall, that is, imagine, fragrances? We may be able to recognize fragrances—you can recognize the scent of the white-and-red candy from the restaurant as peppermint—but can you truly capture the *scent image* of a peppermint in your mind's nose when the candy isn't there? (p. 86)

The answer to Herz's question would depend on how she defines "scent image" as well as the methodology used. Researchers in the *Cognition and Emotion* journal note that many olfactory methodologies, "cannot control for individual differences between memories in terms of content, affective value, and time past since encoding" (Toffolo, Smeets, & van den Hout, 2012, p. 85). Those who answer yes to Herz's question—that they can in fact capture a scent image without the actual odor present—are usually rebuked by those in the natural sciences, and frequently reference neuroimaging studies to support their claims. Herz notes that for vision and hearing, "the same areas of the brain are active during imagining and perceiving a particular sensation," but apparently that is not the case for odors. "The parts of the brain involved in actually smelling pumpkin pie do not overlap neatly with the parts of the brain that are active when you imagine the aroma of pumpkin pie" (2007, pp. 86-87). Thus, according to neuroimaging studies we cannot "truly" imagine an odor, at least not in the same way that we can "visualize" an object in our mind's eye. If we are not actually imagining an odor, what then is taking place? Is it possible that something else is going on in the psyche, something that we cannot yet measure objectively?

Engen's lemon example used earlier claimed that we don't actually smell lemony scent but rather we picture the color and shape of a lemon and how it makes us feel, and therefore believe that we are imagining the fragrance itself. Herz (2007) affirms Engen's ideas when she writes that, "for most people it seems that the sensation of re-creating the image of an aroma is derived from related perceptions and memories" (p. 88), and offers this example:

> Remembering what a turkey looks like, browned and gleaming, as it emerges from the oven; the warmth of the kitchen; a mood of happy satisfaction; and the anticipation of the savory flavors all conjure the *feeling* of smelling turkey at Thanksgiving. But our mind's nose is most likely not experiencing turkey the way we experience it when it is really being carved in front of us. (p. 88)

But do we ever experience a memory the same way we experienced the original event? Are our minds simply a repository or a computer that can precisely re-experience our past? Some smell experts are starting to question the literal accuracy of memory:

> Just as the larger field of memory research has retreated from the notion of indelible flashbulb memory and questioned the veracity of eye-witness testimony, smell experts are recognizing that memory for odor is like memory for anything else—subject to fading, distortion, and misinterpretation. (Gilbert, 2008, p. 204)

Memory is more complex, adds Herz (2007), than it appears. "Memory is more than just an accurate mental presentation of the past. In addition to the facts, like remembering where Grandma lived, memories have a personal, subjective, and emotional dimension" (p. 66). Although Herz does not pursue this line of inquiry more deeply, she is, perhaps unknowingly, edging her way toward the imagination and the soul's way of remembering.

Let us now turn to some thinkers in the field of depth psychology to see if we can better understand the relationship between memory and imagination. Freud was one of the first to venture into another person's psyche and seriously question the reality of memory and fantasy. Hillman (1972) summarizes what Freud discovered.

> The memories Freud collected through his talking cure seemed at first quite plain reminiscences. Memory seemed plainly to be a repository of past events—primarily, traumatic childhood events— but on closer scrutiny these events turned out to be

> not actualities but fantasies. In the world they had
> never happened at all, yet they happened in the
> memory. Memory, therefore, could not be quite so
> plain as it had seemed. It was not only a storehouse
> of what had happened. It also had a fantasy aspect
> that affected present and future. (p. 169)

That our memory is not always accurate, not exactly how it actually happened, is not an easy idea to accept. To admit such a fact would strike a blow to our ego, which likes to believe it has complete control of its experience, including what and how we remember. "But memory often suffers from the disturbing interference of unconscious contents," notes Jung (1939/1969). "Moreover, it functions as a rule automatically" (p. 282). Perhaps this is why the ego tends to literalize memories. Hillman explains it this way:

> It is easier to bear the truth of facts than the truth
> of fantasies; we prefer to literalize memories. For
> to realize that the psyche fabricates memories
> means to accept the reality that experiences
> themselves are being made by the soul out of itself
> and independently of the ego's engagement in its
> so-called real world. (1975, p. 18)

Since, according to Hillman, our experiences are being made by the soul and not only by the mind may perhaps illuminate why it seems so difficult to "accurately" recall a scent image. Furthermore, "we cannot will (*voluntas*) or love (*amor*) or form a notion (*notitia*) or understand (*intelligentia*) without imaginal fantasies going on simultaneously" (1972, p. 177). In other words, our imagination is influencing all areas of our human experience. "Memory not only records, it also confabulates, that is, it makes up imaginary happenings, wholly psychic events" (1975, p. 18). Let us also hear the simple but profound words of Bachelard (1960/1969): "The past is not stable; it does not return to the memory either with the same traits or in the same light…the soul and the mind do not have the same memory" (p. 104).

Thus, even if a particular scent vividly transports us back in time, and we re-experience all the associated memories and emotions, the scent memory will be colored by the soul's imagination. "I never smell daisies without living over again the ecstatic mornings that my teacher and I spent wandering in the fields, while I learned new words and the names of things" (Keller, 2009, p. 26). The "living over again" is done in and through our imagination. Cowan (2002) offers another way of looking at the memory of the mind and the soul:

> Psychological history is different from literal history, in that it is a collection of images made from subjective experience and not exclusively from external events. It is the difference between an impressionist's painting and a journalist's photograph. Memory and imagination go together; the one is hardly possible without the other. (p. 62)

If we liken the mind's memory to a journalist's photograph, we must admit that even a photograph portrays only one viewpoint, one particular angle in a single moment in time. Thus, even the mind's memory does not capture the whole scene. Cowan writes that psychological, or soul history has the characteristic of an impressionist's painting, a collection of internal images. I would take it one step further and say that it is like an impressionist's painting that is constantly shifting and moving, one that cannot be hung securely on a wall. For all memories are only experienced now, in the present moment, and whatever state our psyches happen to be in will shape both the present and the past.

> What today we conventionally refer to as memory is *imagining qualified by time*. When we are recollecting, we are always imagining, even if what comes up is placed back in time. The sole difference between imagining and imagination on the one hand, and remembering and memory on the other is this added element of time. (Hillman, 1999, p. 89)

I recently made oatmeal lace cookies from an old family recipe. The delicious scents of oats, butter, and brown sugar brought me back to my childhood. My father used to make these cookies fairly often, so happy images of him began to come forth. I stood in my kitchen eating the cookies with a friend while I reflected on pleasant childhood memories. My friend pointed out that not everyone has happy memories of childhood. I agreed and then thought about times when my parents argued loudly in the kitchen, sometimes due to my father making a mess of the kitchen. At that moment the smell of the cookies gave me a different feeling, one that was not quite as pleasant. "In this remote region, memory and imagination remain associated, each one working for their mutual deepening. In the order of values, they both constitute a community of memory and image" (Bachelard, 1958/1994, p. 5). The relationship between imagination and memory is not simple, each influencing the other depending on the needs, desires, and tendencies of the psyche. If the scent of the cookies had the potential to carry both joyous and unpleasant associations, perhaps my initial bias toward pleasant memories was stronger than my need to imagine the unpleasant ones?

From examples used thus far and what we know from olfactory research, it is easier and more emotionally intense to experience scent memories when an actual odorant infiltrates our nose and brain. "Ironically, though odors are exceptional triggers of memory, it is extremely difficult, if not impossible, to summon up the memory of an odor itself" (Herz, 2007, p. 85). Even a great dreamer such as Bachelard (1958/1994) admits the need for a strong imagination to recapture an odor memory:

> I alone, in my memories of another century, can open the deep cupboard that still retains for me alone that unique odor, the odor of raisins drying on a wicker tray. The odor of raisins! It is an odor that is beyond description, one that it takes a lot of imagination to smell. (p. 13)

The scent of drying raisins is a poignant memory, yet Bachelard is surprisingly at a loss for words in describing the aroma and notes the amount of work needed to recall it. Imagining a fragrance is not easy, but it is not impossible. Gilbert (2008) is confident this is a skill that we can learn. "At the core of olfactory imagination is skill at mental imagery. We can bring to mind an odor the same way we imagine a visual scene" (p. 131).

Though Gilbert's statement contradicts Herz's findings, I think it is important to at least propose that, with practice, we can improve our olfactory imagination. Keller (2009) no doubt had significant practice: "Even as I think of smells, my nose is full of scents that start awake sweet memories of summers gone and ripening grain fields far away" (p. 27). I suspect that the acts of reverie, daydreaming, and reminiscing on certain scents strengthens our imagination and polishes the inner smellscape. Let us slow down a moment and listen yet again to the words of Bachelard (1960/1969):

> Odors! The first evidence of our fusion with the world. These memories of odors from the past are recovered by closing our eyes. Long ago we closed our eyes to savor them fully. We closed our eyes and then, right away, we dreamed a little. By dreaming well, by dreaming simply in a tranquil reverie, we are going to find them again. (p. 136)

It may simply be the case that to imagine fragrances, to find them again, we need to practice closing our eyes, taking deep breaths, and letting ourselves dream freely.

For the past decade or so I have been reliving a very peculiar scent by imagining and pondering upon it. It is the smell of being inside the barrel of an ocean wave. For a surfer one of the most enjoyable experiences is to be covered within the hollow tube created by the curling lip of a wave. During the few seconds inside a barrel there is a mist that is sometimes created by the pressure of the water and air. This mist usually smells of salt, seaweed, and some kind of mineral like copper (depending on which beach I surf). I have never smelled anything else exactly like it, so it has always held my curiosity since I was a kid. As my obsession with smells grew I found myself daydreaming about it. As Guerer (1992) notes, "dreaming or reverie allows us to recapture the odors in which memories lie encapsulated" (p. 200). With practice it is now a scent that is not difficult for me to imagine, despite several months passing since I last inhaled the barrel mist.

The old expression, "use it or lose it," may indeed be appropriate here. If we stop smelling things, dismiss scent memories when they arise, and cease daydreaming, it is likely our olfactory and imaginative abilities will severely decline. "Since imagination affects memory and perception, what distinguishes old taste connoisseurs from other seniors dependent on taste enhancers may be not the quantity of their taste buds but their still freshly budding imagining powers" (Hillman, 1999, p. 115). Without continual practice our imagination can wither as much as our skin and nasal epithelium.

In addition to practice, let us recall our need for aesthetics. We need to smell and remember and imagine images of beauty. "The beauty of soul which alone surpasses the allure of Aphrodite will show in the aesthetic imagination of the psyche and the attractive power of its images" (Hillman, 1972, p. 101). We are back to images, the substance of our psyches, the living presences that move our being and fill and nourish our lives. We must praise not only beautiful scent images but also the images that perturb and disturb us, regardless of whether they come from the mind's or the soul's memory:

> A life full of all kinds of memory images—ugly memories, joyful memories, sorrowful and painful memories, funny and embarrassing and ridiculous memories, sensate memories of how some things felt even when it can't be remembered how it actually was, or if it ever *really* was. In the course of psychic life, literal events by themselves count for relatively little. (Cowan, 2002, p. 67)

If, like Cowan proclaims, the psyche gives literal events in our life less weight, we must be vigilant and not place absolute faith in literal, time-specific scent memories. To keep our aesthetic heart in a state of expansion we must continue to dream. As Hillman (1975) writes:

> The soul has shrunk because its imagination has withered, and so we have little psychological space for fantasying, for holding things and mulling, for letting be. Events pass right through us, traceless. Or they press us into tight corners, no room to maneuver, no inner distance. We can hold more in mind than in soul, so that the contents of our minds are largely without psychological significance, input without digestion. (p. 93)

Our inner smellscape can contract or expand depending on how much attention and quality time we spend pondering and reflecting on our scent memories. To prevent our souls from shrinking, as Hillman observed, we might do well to cultivate a more intimate relationship with our images. This may increase psychic space and allow our scent images more fluidity, so that they do not get stuck in a fixed form or chained to the past. As Cowan reminds us:

> It is important that we learn to remember forwardly as well as remembering what is past…there is an art to remembering forwardly, to anticipating with passion what one can be or do in life. It requires an image, or many images. (2002, pp. 66-67)

What beautiful and disgusting scent images are yet to be discovered? What scents will be re-discovered, perhaps the same aromas our ancestors inhaled? Yet we each have our own peculiar, idiosyncratic scent images and our own ways of poetically sharing them:

> Part of the soul is continually remembering in mythopoetic speech, continually seeing, feeling, and hearing *sub specie aeternitatis*. Experience reverberates with memories, and it echoes reminiscences that we may never actually have lived. Thereby our lives seem at one and the same moment to be uniquely our own and altogether new, yet to carry an ancestral aura, a quality of *déjà vu*. (Hillman, 1972, p. 177)

That our scent experiences echo and reverberate, confabulating what we thought was literal and exact, gives testimony to the reality of our imagination and its power to form and deform images. To me this is a fascinating phenomenon that requires careful consideration and reflection. These ideas will be developed more fully in the next chapter on meaning and reflection.

We began this chapter on language and the difficult but necessary task of skillfully and poetically describing our scent experiences. We saw how integral our breath is to smelling and its relationship with beauty and aesthetics. The importance of context was made apparent to help us better understand how ugly and beautiful scent images are created. A deepening into certain pleasant and unpleasant scent memories was undertaken, which ultimately lead us in the direction of the imagination and its important role in memory. I will end this chapter with a quote from Cowan (2002) which summarizes where we have been and points to where we are headed: "In attending to the soul's deepest need, the essential question is not so much *what* I remember, but *how* I remember it…to redeem the memory image means to find meaning in it" (p. 60). We are now at the point where we must step back and reflect on our meaningful scent images.

Chapter 5

SMELL YOUR REFLECTIONS: THE MIRRORS OF MEANING

Though pool-reflections may swim
blurred from the surface, know the image.
~R. M. Rilke, *"The Sonnets to Orpheus"*

The trees are in their autumn beauty,
The woodland paths are dry,
Under the October twilight the water
Mirrors a still sky
~W.B. Yeats, *"The Wild Swans at Coole"*

Letting one second go on
To go over a lifetime
We were such good friends
Will you find me where I am now?
~Katatonia, *"Second"*

I recently attended a high school football game. As I watched the action from the bleachers I started to have memories of playing football over twenty years ago. With nostalgia I recalled all the hot afternoons of practice: running, hitting, yelling, and laughing. I observed passively as my psyche poured forth images of night games, conversations on the bus when we traveled to away games, working out in the gym, and team meetings. My imagination then came upon the locker room. I saw myself putting on my pads and uniform, observed images of my teammates bantering and taking showers. Then came the smells.

The locker room at my school was old and so carried years of use (and abuse) by male teens. I recalled the smell of musty walls and moldy tiles, wooden benches, porcelain sinks and tap water, metallic locker doors and padlocks. I inhaled the pleasant aromas of grass and soil that our cleats tracked in, which contrasted with the scents of my teammates' deodorant and over-applied, cheap cologne. But the odor that stood out most was sweat. It was as if the sweat of thousands of teenage boys over decades had permeated every inch of the locker room. The sweat under our helmets, sweat soaked in our jerseys and pads, plus our individual body odor (some guys smelled worse than others)—each kind of sweat had subtle differences. When I was in high school I mildly disliked the odor of locker room sweat. But now in my mid 30s, as I sat watching other teens play, I experienced the locker room scent image with a feeling of pleasantness. My body felt charged with energy, as if it was ready to run out on the field to play. More, I felt filled with meaning as I started to comprehend just how important playing high school football was to me.

As I now reflect on these memories it is as if the odor of my football locker room carried a whole constellation of emotions, memories, and fantasies—in other words, a meaningful smellscape. The deeper I reflect the more I see and understand how the locker room scent image carries much of my youth: pride of my athletic body, of friendship, fighting, insecurities and growing confidence in my ability to physically hit and be hit. The shared experience with my teammates was also built into the scent of the locker room. The years of struggle, injuries, excitement, putdowns and encouragements—all encapsulated by the complex aroma of my football locker room. This is an inner smellscape that is rich with images, one that for me is weighty and full of significance.

The Who and What of Reflection

Narcissus vanished. All that remained
was the fragrance of his beauty—
constant and sweet, the scent of heliotrope.
His task was only to behold himself.
~R.M. Rilke, *"Narcissus"*

We are but the images of those we've
loved—
and they?
Images, too, of lost beloveds.
Image reflecting image. On and on...
~Christine Downing, *"Narcissus Reflections"*

From mirror after mirror
No vanity's displayed:
I'm looking for the face I had
Before the world was made.
~W.B. Yeats, *"Before the World was Made"*

Who determines what makes a scent image meaningful? Who is it that reflects upon certain scent images while ignoring others? I am concerned here with investigating the subject, the one who inhales aromas, feels emotions, notices memory images arise, and reflects upon this whole experience. When I ask people this question, the answer I most often hear is an obvious "I do" or "me." Who is this "I"? This question requires a deeper inquiry.

I wish to start with Jung (1928/1969) who wrote extensively on the structure and function of the psyche:

> Since man appears to be a living unity in himself, the conclusion would follow that the images of all his psychic activities are united in one total image of the whole man, which if known to him would be regarded as an ego. (p. 325)

Jung is stating that what we commonly refer to as "I" or "me" can also be called ego. We wake up in the morning and say, "I slept well," or "I had many dreams." The part of the psyche that says this, Jung proposed, is the ego. To put it another way, "the term ego refers to one's experience of oneself as a center of willing, desiring, reflecting, and acting" (Stein, 2015, p. 15).

The ego is what Jung (1951/1959) sometimes called the "empirical personality" (p. 3). The ego can be thought of as the focal point of our awareness, that which filters and controls our daily activities. All conscious contents are related to the ego. This is because no content within the psyche can be conscious without a subject to apprehend it. "By ego I understand a complex of ideas which constitutes the center of my field of consciousness and appears to possess a high degree of continuity and identity," writes Jung (1923/1971, p. 425). Thus, the sense of being me, an embodied and separate entity that thinks, feels, and acts willfully, is understood to be an ego. In sum, "the ego is the subject of all personal acts of consciousness" (1951/1959, p. 3).

If, however, following Jung (1928/1969), we make the statement that the ego is only part of the psyche, it implies that there are other parts within us, that there is more to who we are than the "empirical personality." Jung elaborates: "The ego is a complex that does not comprise the total human being; it has forgotten infinitely more than it knows. It has heard and seen an infinite amount of which it has never become conscious" (p. 324). As we have touched upon in previous sections, there is much in our lives that we are not conscious of, a part of reality that remains below the surface of our conscious awareness. For instance, we have discovered from the olfactory research that many of our scent associations and memories are formed automatically and unconsciously. We often do not know of our hedonic feelings toward certain aromas until we smell them, whereupon our ego is confronted with the odorant's impact upon us.

A scent image or any other psychic content must come into association with the ego for the content to become conscious. As Jung (1928/1969) points out, "if there is no such association, it remains unconscious. Forgetfulness shows how often and how easily contents lose their connection with the ego" (p. 323). Attentive awareness is therefore an important characteristic of the ego as the center of our psyche. "The ego is responsible for retaining contents in consciousness," notes Stein (2015), "and it can also eliminate contents from consciousness by ceasing to reflect them" (p. 18). Our ego must be able and willing to hold psychic images in its awareness. "This interior personality, subject to the control of remembering, can, in Augustine's words, bring forth and drive away images 'with the hand of my heart'" (Hillman, 1975, p. 196).

Perhaps the ego could be likened to a flashlight or magnifying glass, which brings into focus only that which its lens and light beam illuminates. Jung sometimes wrote that the ego functions like a mirror within the psyche, which may be a more precise analogy. The ego, Jung (1928/1969) asserts, "can be understood as an image or reflection of all the activities comprehended by it" (p. 325). Elsewhere he writes that the ego is "made up of images recorded from the sense-functions that transmit stimuli both from within and from without, and furthermore of an immense accumulation of images of past processes" (1928/1969, p. 323). Stein (2015) summarizes Jung's thinking:

> The ego is a kind of mirror in which the psyche can see itself and can become aware. The degree to which a psychic content is taken up and reflected by the ego is the degree to which it can be said to belong to the realm of consciousness. When a psychic content is only vaguely or marginally conscious, it has not yet been captured and held in place upon the ego's reflective surface. (p. 15)

We cannot see our own eyes except by looking into a mirror, having our eyes photographed, or through a video recording. Hillman (1975) offers a similar metaphor: "Glass is the metaphor par excellence for psychic reality: it is itself not visible, appearing only to be its contents" (p. 142). As it is with our outer physical eyes, so too the psyche needs an inner mirror—an ego—in order to see itself. Hillman also points out that "Picasso, who was a painter, understood his life as multiple self-portraits in facing mirrors, images of himself that did not narrate a story through time. He said: 'I don't develop. I am'" (1978, pp. 160-161). Perhaps each face or figure of our psyche has a different relationship to certain scents, along with each figure's memories and associations. For instance, the "young boy" part of me still loves the smell of a candy store, while the "old man" figure savors the aroma of whiskey.

In response to my question above—who does the reflective act—I propose, following Jung, that it is a mirror-like structure within our psyche called the ego. It is our ego that can reflect on scent images, or just as easily, dismiss and ignore these images. As Hanna (1970) correctly points out: "Only occasionally does one self-consciously reflect on anything at all" (p. 43). What we reflect on, how much or how often we reflect, and the style or type of reflection depends primarily on the ego itself.

I would like to give another concrete example to complement the preceding theoretical and philosophical paragraphs. Last week one of my patients told me about an experience she had at an outdoor garden store. While shopping for plants, she walked past employees sawing some kind of wood. She told me the smell of the cut wood arrested her for a moment, as something inside her was taking shape. There was something familiar about the scent but she couldn't quite place it. The feeling in her body was warm and gentle but she could feel her lungs contracting with a touch of unknown nostalgia. She continued walking around and about twenty minutes later images started to form. She saw scenes of the backyard of her childhood home, then images of her father in his work shed. She said her father used to make furniture as an occasional hobby. The smell she recognized was a certain type of wood her father used to use. She was surprised because she had forgotten that her father used to enjoy woodworking. He was a scientist and was known more for his intellect. She spent the rest of the afternoon engaged with childhood memories, especially of her father, many of which she hadn't thought about in years.

This example illustrates how content from the unconscious must come into association with a subject (an ego) for the content to become conscious. Had she not paused and paid attention to the scent and allowed images to rise into her awareness, the memory images would have remained unconscious. Further, it was her ego, I propose, that later reflected on her scent experience and subsequent images and memories that had been constellated.

The ability to self-reflect is one characteristic that humans possess. But are all acts of reflection the same? Do different kinds of reflection influence or determine what we see or don't see, notice or don't notice? Berry (2008) offers one explanation:

> Frames organize what we see. Organized well, what we see can become fresh, even breathtaking. The way in which a picture is framed becomes part of its effect and meaning…the purpose of framing is to put limits on the view so that what is within those limits can be focused on with greater clarity and freshness. (p. 185)

In making this comment, Berry is alluding to the possibility of different styles of reflection. If we use the analogy of a camera, the act of reflection can take place by the ego either zooming out or zooming in on psychic contents. In general, zooming out places psychic contents into a context. This gives us a wider frame that allows contents to be seen and understood in relationship to each other and in relationship to the external environment. In contrast, the act of zooming in is more intimate and is concerned with details and specifics. Both are possible modes of reflection depending on how we want or need to frame our images and experiences. Each way tells a slightly different story. Let us investigate these two ways of reflection.

Reflection by Zooming Out

We evaporate or we condense—
we dream or we think.
If only we could always imagine!
~Gaston Bachelard, *Air and Dreams*

There is a harmony in the bending back, as in
the case of the bow and the lyre.
~Heraclitus

The senses perceive objects of sense, but the
mind alone can compare them.
~Socrates

Before outlining the two modes of reflection, I wish to briefly present the typical ideas of reflection in American and European thinking. Western philosophy has traditionally conceptualized the act of reflection to be abstract, detached, objective, and impersonal. Observe a passage from the prominent philosopher, Schopenhauer (2010):

> It is noteworthy, indeed marvelous, that we human beings always lead a second, abstract life alongside our concrete life. In the first we are subject to all the storms of reality and are prey to the influence of the present: we must strive, suffer and die, just as animals do. But our abstract life, as it appears before us in rational contemplation, is the calm reflection of the first life and the world it is lived in…In this realm of peaceful deliberation what had previously possessed us completely and moved us deeply, now appears cold, colorless and strange to the eye: here we are simply onlookers and spectators. In this retreat into reflection we are like actors who have played our scene, and now take our seats among the audience before we have to return to the stage; anything may now happen on the stage, even the preparation of our own death, and, looking out from the audience, we view it with equanimity; but then we return to act and suffer as we must. (p. 112)

Schopenhauer is pointing out a common human dialectic between concrete and abstract experience. His idea of reflection as "rational contemplation" is cold and detached. As seen in the context of human development this is quite an achievement. "The whole history of cultural evolution can be seen as a great *sublimatio* process in which human beings learn how to see themselves and their world objectively" (Edinger, 1994, p. 125).

Unfortunately, over time the words "objective" and "rational" have come to be associated with qualities such as impersonal, unemotional, and detached. If I were to use western philosophy's ideas of reflection, I would be straying far from the core of my research on meaningful scent images. For my research has demonstrated that each person has his or her own idiosyncratic scent images. These images are personally meaningful, embodied, derived from concrete life experiences, and tend to be emotionally charged. Reflection therefore should be undertaken in a similar manner. In other words, rather than seeing the act of reflection as a detached intellectual pursuit lacking emotion, I am keeping with the thrust of my research by maintaining a phenomenological and somatic stance on reflection.

I propose that a zooming-out style of reflection creates context. This context allows us to observe the relationship between the personal and the collective, between our idiosyncratic scent images and our cultural and historical lives in which they are embedded. Zooming out also engenders a kind of distance or space in which the relationship between the ego and the images in the psyche can be recognized.

The reflective act of zooming out thus involves situating scent images and their associations within a cultural and historical context. This mode of reflection gives us a wider and more inclusive perspective. For instance, I have a scent image from my childhood of eating strawberries from my neighbor's garden. When I reflect on the scent of strawberry, I sometimes think about the fact that synthetic strawberry fragrances have become ubiquitous in the United States and Europe. One large corporation—Givaudan—makes 6,000 versions of "strawberry flavor" alone (Herz, 2007, p. 200). From yogurt to candles to soap, manufactured strawberry scent has become so common that many kids (and some adults) do not know what an actual strawberry even smells like. This wasn't the case seventy-five years ago. My grandparents knew the aroma of strawberry exclusively from the fruit. Thus, when I notice any of my scent images that involve strawberry aroma, I can understand them within a cultural and historical context.

Since zooming out brings forth a bigger picture, there is space in which to see our personal scent images in relationship to the collective. From this many insights and connections may arise. But, as Casey notes, this kind of reflection requires time and patience:

> There must be a stage of retention—not in the usual memory sense of holding in mind explicitly, but of its holding some position in space and time so you can pursue it, develop it, exfoliate it, you know, go *with* it—all of that. (as cited in Hillman, 2016b, p. 409)

We must be willing to take time to view our scent images respectfully. To be curious and thoughtful in our reflections may help us see how fragrances are conceptualized in our culture over time. As an example, let us take a common American aroma: popcorn. When I zoom out from that particular fragrance, I see generations of people at the movie theaters sharing in collective experiences. But I also witness the manipulation of movie theaters as they pump popcorn scent outside the theater to attract customers. I also think about the invention of microwave popcorn, which sharply increased popcorn consumption across the country, beginning in the 1970s. Microwave popcorn also coincided with a new generation of people who do not go to the movie theaters but instead watch movies at home. This leads me to further reflect on the adverse health consequences due to the use of microwaves. This idea leads me to imagine our ancestors thousands of years ago popping corn from wood fires and how different the scent must have been compared to what we experience today.

Because zooming out creates context, there is a wider frame in which to view interrelated images, memories, and ideas. Often one idea or memory leads to another and can go on this way for some time. Hillman (2016f) likens this experience to a good conversation, which he says reverberates long after it is over. "It keeps on talking in your mind later in the day...That reverberation afterwards is the very raising of consciousness: your mind's been moved. You are at another level with your reflections" (p. 38). For instance, I was sitting at the beach recently and I caught a whiff of very strong perfume. About one hundred yards away a woman was walking near the shore, and since there was no one else close by, I determined the perfume came from her. I was immediately irritated that natural sea aromas were interrupted by the dense, overly sweet odor from this woman. The smell lingered for a couple minutes then eventually dissipated. Over the next several hours I ruminated on the scent. I couldn't help but think of the billion-dollar perfume industry, which encourages people to drench themselves in synthetic chemical fragrances. I thought of the ancient Egyptians, who were one of the first cultures to use natural perfumes. Humans have been masking or altering their body odor for centuries. But only in the last century did we start wearing synthetic fragrances. Generally, for me, chemical perfumes and colognes are too strong and irritating to my body, often initiating a headache. Some people wear just a little perfume that is subtle, but more often than not they are all too much for me. When I encounter such intense perfume, I usually plug my nose, shake my head, and think, "Why?" It seems so unnecessary to wear such outrageous fragrances.

Scent images and our associations and insights may reverberate when we stay committed to this style of reflection. It may only take one striking odor to initiate such a reflective disposition. As Bachelard (1958/1994) writes, "after the original reverberation, we are able to experience resonances, sentimental repercussions, reminders of our past" (p. xxiii). The phrase, "sentimental repercussions," conjures for me the experience of one feeling leading to another, or one scent memory sparking an associated idea or mood. Thus, zooming out creates a context in which memories, ideas, and images echo and reverberate, showing the relationship between the individual and the collective.

Another benefit of zooming out is that it gives space to see the relationship between the ego and the images in the psyche. There are some occasions where we do not consciously choose to ponder and reflect on our meaningful scent images. Sometimes scent memories intrude into our awareness, asserting their own autonomous nature, demanding to be recognized and understood. As an example, I recently walked by a Carl's Jr. fast food restaurant. My first reaction to the smell coming from the place was of disgust. To me the odor signifies a business that serves nasty, unhealthy, and unethical food and drink. I began to walk faster to avoid the stench. Yet as I continued my walk, I started to feel a sense of nostalgia for Carl's Jr., as a multitude of surprisingly pleasant memory images of my youth arose. In high school I used to go there for lunch with my football friends, and when I was in the Boy Scouts we would sometimes eat there on our road trips. Despite my current disdain for the greasy, sweet, and overly seasoned food, my ego watched the images with a kind of mild fascination. Did I really used to eat double bacon western cheeseburgers and drink large Dr. Pepper sodas? My ego felt some guilt for eating so unhealthy as a teenager, but also maintained an attitude of forgiveness and amusement for having been young and ignorant.

Although it had been over a decade since I had last eaten there, the scent memories associated with the odor of Carl's Jr. appeared to my ego crisp and vivacious. Our psyche holds an enormous amount of past images from our life, yet when our ego watches and reflects on these images they sometimes appear to be quite fresh and alive. "What one takes to be new and originary is actually already the echo of an immemorial past, that the present is freighted with memories" (Shamdasani & Hillman, 2013, p. 227). Reflection by zooming out provides enough psychic space for our egos to come into a relationship with images from both the present and the past—perhaps the future as well.

In brief, the zooming out style of reflection creates context. This context allows us to observe the relationship between our personal scent images and our culture, over time. Zooming out also lets us see the correspondence between the ego and the images in the psyche. Now let us zoom in and investigate another style of reflection.

Reflection by Zooming In

If anyone wants to know what "spirit" is,
or what "God's fragrance" means,
lean your head toward him or her
Keep your face there close
Like this
~Rumi, *The Essential Rumi*

It is in the act itself, lived as a unified whole,
that dynamic imagination must be able to
experience the double human destiny
of depth and height.
~Gaston Bachelard, *Air and Dreams*

If somebody drew them into sleep, slept deep
with those things—how light he would be, and
different, coming to the new day
from this mutual depth.
~R. M. Rilke, *"The Sonnets to Orpheus, Pt. Two"*

In contrast to zooming out, reflection by zooming in captures subtle details and particular qualities of psychic contents. Zooming in therefore engenders a feeling of intimacy and closeness. Our meaningful scent images come into sharp focus as we reflect and attend to their unique characteristics. Hillman (1979a) calls this style of reflection "close noticing":

> As well as Apollonic reflection (leaning back and
> away, distancing), there is another sort of attention,
> moving closer to sniff, discrimination with the
> eyes closed as in music and prayer and kissing, as
> in remembering. Close noticing. This approach to
> living psychologically reconnects us to the ancient
> meaning of *psyche* as breath-soul of the head
> whose passages were the nostrils. (p. 143)

Hillman is suggesting a type of reflection in which we are
drawn toward psychic contents with respectful attention, a
move that is even devotional perhaps. It is as if we enter
the smellscape and can see and feel each particular detail.
For instance, I smell the flowers of a trumpet vine and I
am back in the alley behind my childhood home. I can see
the weeds, the bees, lizards, and the way the sun reflects
on my friends long brown hair. I hear the chatter of ten-
year-olds, excited to lick the sweet liquid from the flower
stems. "Rather than reflection through distance, the image
here is intimate, reflective sensitivity, Athena in the
touch" (Berry, 2008, pp. 145-146). With zooming in we
are not interested in the cultural or historical context of
our scent images, but rather in their personal and
particular characteristics.

A consequence of "close noticing" is the
engendering of intimacy. For example, if we look at a
person and notice only their gender, height, and hair
color—surface characteristics—we rarely feel anything
special about them; there is a lack of intimacy. If,
however, we pay attention to the way in which they move
their hands, notice what the back of their neck smells like,
and pick up subtle inflections of their voice, we may feel
we know the person more deeply. In a similar way we can

experience our psychic images by zooming in, which gives us a feeling of closeness. In other words, the ego becomes more intimate with the images of the psyche.

Let us recall that the act of smelling is itself an intimate encounter. Odorants in our environment must reach the olfactory receptors in our nose for us to smell anything at all. As Herz (2007) points out, "olfactory receptors, unlike the receptors in any other sensory system, are directly exposed to the outside world, which is why among other things we can inhale drugs" (p. 20). We may see or hear a person at a fair distance, but we must be physically close to be able to smell them. The zooming into our smellscape has this same kind of intimacy. It is less an intellectual activity, but more of an attentive noticing. "We can become intimate with an image or a thing in a sensuous way only when we have abandoned the rational account of it. Intimacy…depends on the experience of the particular as such" (Hillman, 2014, p. 56). Reflection by zooming out engages the intellect in an attempt to understand how a personal scent image fits or relates to culture and history. This is not the case with zooming in; no such thinking needs to take place. It is more of an embodied experience, a phenomenological experience. Our imagination comes to life and stirs the images and we experience them immediately, sensuously.

Let me offer an example. Oscar was a mutt we had in my family for fifteen years. I have attempted to recollect his scent but have found it difficult, as it has been many years since he died. So, I began to reflect on other parts of him to bring his scent closer. I imagined touching his fur, hearing his whines and barks, and seeing him run at the beach. There were hundreds of memory images and slowly I began to smell him. I could actually differentiate a variety of his scents. For instance, after he had a bath, after he had been lying in the sun, and a few horrid occasions he rolled joyously in a dead bird or fish at the beach. The more I contacted other sensory details in my imagination the more I could sniff and breathe—take in—his doggy scent. Once again, I felt right there next to him, bending down to scratch his neck, then sticking my own face in his chest to snuggle in a simple moment of intimacy. "'Taking in' means taking to heart, interiorizing, becoming intimate with" (Hillman, 2014, p. 40).

In this kind of reflective experience there is less a sense of spaciousness and distance but rather a sense of tightness and precision. There even seems to be an actual leaning forward of my body as I engage in intimate reflection. As Bachelard (1958/1994) observes, "there does not exist a real intimacy that is repellent. All the spaces of intimacy are designated by an attraction" (p. 12). It is this attraction that keeps us moving closer toward our scent images. Lockhart (1987) elaborates this idea:

> Most of the images we experience in our everyday life keep us moving always away from what we have just seen. In this moving away there is a kind of forgetting. But a photograph rivets us to the spot, forcing us into memory, forcing a movement of psyche. To fix the image, as for example in focusing on the image in a dream, is an eros act that awakens psyche and initiates psyche's movement. We stop this psychic movement only when we move away from a photograph or an image or passively letting the images go by us. (p. 28)

Lockhart is suggesting a style of attention that awakens our heart in an act of appreciation to whatever is presented to our ego. "This thought of the heart returns us to an animal thought, intimacy released from confession into immediacy, the courage of immediate intimacy, and not merely with ourselves, but with the particular faces of the sensate world" (Hillman, 2014, p. 57). It is as if zooming in toward our scent images helps us to remember them more deeply, and by remembering the details and particulars of the image we therefore feel a greater intimacy and connection to those images. Bachelard (1960/1969) again: "In the past as in the present, a beloved odor is the center of an intimacy. Some memories are faithful to this intimacy" (p. 136). It is natural to give our devoted attention to that which we adore.

Like certain people, animals, objects, and places we love, a scent can indeed feel like a beloved. We could even go far and say that some scents are incorporated into our identity. At the very least zooming in on our scent images brings us closer to our own soul. "When going into the imagination, it seems one should keep close to the images… 'Know thyself' means also know thy peculiar images, holding them in an interior void, close and familiar, without doing anything to them or for them" (Hillman, 1975, pp. 93-94). To know and feel our idiosyncratic scent images is like seeing ourselves deeply through our own eyes when peering into a mirror. In this case we need not do anything more than be present to what appears in our psyche. There is no need to analyze, interpret, compare, or categorize the images. We can, like with a captivating movie, lean in toward the screen and simply enjoy the show.

It is worth remarking that zooming in does not simply leave us on the surface of mere appearances. No, we can indeed peer deeply into a smellscape by leaning in and reflecting on particular details:

> As the eye watching a picture both concentrates and darts, so the mind confronted with an image starts racing even as it stands still. This double action discloses levels and builds complexities without ever leaving the scene, without ever going beyond the dumb object with which it is presented. Like a picture, an image too has borders. It sticks to itself, inheres within itself. It doesn't lead somewhere else, as does a story. Thus the mind's activity can find nowhere to go but more deeply into the image. (Hillman, 1978, p. 160)

Another way of deepening into an image is through repetition. To go over the same scent image, even in an obsessional way, can yield a feeling of intimacy and fullness of meaning. "We repeat what we find self-reflectively beautiful. Narcissus longs deeply for (or longs to deepen) the beauty of this self-reflection. His longing is downward into the pool, toward his reflection in depth" (Berry, 2008, p. 112). There have been times in my life where I have felt the longing of home and safety. One scent image that brings me comfort is of the pasta my mom used to cook. Once when I was traveling alone in southern Italy as a young adult, I got misdirected on the train, headed in the wrong direction. I remember thinking of "home" as a way to assuage my anxiety of being lost. One memory image that continued to arise in my psyche was my mom's penne pasta with fresh basil. I could feel the warm food and house, the voices of my loving family, and many other details from my home. For several hours the pasta-scent image, among others, held fast, as the associations the images brought with them were a welcomed solace.

Yet let us not forget that we not only repeat that which we find desirable, erotic, and meaningful, but also what we dislike, fear, and hate; some repetitive images in our psyche are not pleasant or beautiful. A soldier, for instance, may be unable to turn away from horrible memories and scent images of the stench of burning bodies. In this case repetition of an image is involuntary but nevertheless still caries import. Hillman (1983a) explains, "if that repetition, that rhythm doesn't deepen by return, if it doesn't turn by return, if it doesn't revision, or echo, then there is something merely obsessional. But the obsession is an attempt to get to that deepening" (p. 22). There are important details in unpleasant scent images and therefore much we can gain from careful attending to these images.

It is as if we zoom in toward an image again and again until we see it clearly or understand it more deeply. Or perhaps there is no "until," for "the depth of an image, like that of a psyche, is endless" (Hillman, 1978, p. 158). If we pay close attention to the idiosyncratic details of our scent images, we may feel a sense of depth and fullness. Thus, we reflect by zooming in to know our images more precisely, to gain a feeling of intimacy so that we know ourselves more clearly. Together with the reflective act of zooming out, this can ultimately bring us the experience of meaningfulness.

Mirrors of Meaning

*The psyche, as a reflection of the world
and man, is a thing of such infinite complexity
that it can be observed and studied
from a great many sides.*
~C.G. Jung, *The Structure of the Psyche*

*There's no hiding the fragrance
that comes from an ecstatic.
A polished mirror cannot help reflecting*
~Rumi, *The Essential Rumi*

*To look at one night is like looking in a mirror
containing the reflections
of all the nights that ever were.*
~Wallace Stevens, *Letters*

*Late one December evening I am taking a walk
with a friend. The air is cold and the moon is full and
bright. As we turn a corner along the path a fragrance
catches my attention. I tilt my face and begin to sniff the
air in short rapid bursts. I make a soft moan of pleasure.
Before I have a chance to identify the smell mentally or
verbally, my friend exclaims, "Brian! It's woodchips!"
She nudges me to the side of the path toward an indistinct
dark mound. In a moment we are standing at the base of a
large pile of woodchips. We look at each other a moment
as we realize without saying much that we both love the
scent of woodchips. "I don't know why I love this smell,
but I do. I have for many years," she says. "Wait...I think*

the reason is because my first boyfriend worked as a forest ranger and he used to come home from work with this smell. So, for me it's an aphrodisiac. It wasn't for him, though; strangely, for him the smell of gasoline was an aphrodisiac." I tell her that for me the aroma of woodchips mostly reminds me of my formative years in the Boy Scouts and the many adventurous campouts I had. Before continuing our walk, we each take several deep inhales from the mound, as if trying to savior both our past and this present moment. After a few minutes we stop and sit on a large rock and gaze at the moon through the thin trees. We enter deep into conversation, reflecting on our life path and where we are now. All the while I keep thinking how amusing and beautiful it is to share such a strong feeling of pleasure for the scent of woodchips, though for different reasons. At that moment I breathe deep, inhaling the scent of damp soil and leaves, sycamore trees, and a faint salty-fish scent from the ocean a few miles away. I also smell my friend's unique scent, which is a rich, musty-grape aroma. I feel warm internally despite the cold night. My friend and I both feel and voice our deep appreciation for Nature and its variety of sights, sounds, and smells. We sit in silence staring at the moon, breathing together. No time...

Thus far we have looked at the idea of reflection from the standpoint of the subject—the person doing the internal observing—as well as two types or styles of this reflection. This is important because, as Jung proposes, "a full account of reality must include the presence of the human psyche—the observer—and the element of meaning" (as cited in Stein, 2015, p. 214). My discussion on reflection is in fact leading toward the essential experience of meaningfulness. Ultimately, I am interested in personal scent images that are meaningful to the human psyche. In other words, we need to investigate the elements that make certain inner smellscapes meaningful. Let us start once again with Jung (1923/1971):

> The inner image is a complex structure made up of the most varied material from the most varied sources. It is no conglomerate, however, but a homogeneous product with a meaning of its own. The image is a *condensed expression of the psychic situation as a whole,* and not merely, nor even predominately, of unconscious contents pure and simple. (p. 442)

I believe an "inner image" as a complex structure is similar to how we have used the phrase "inner smellscape." Following Jung's idea, there may be many components and features of the inner smellscape, but there is a feeling of wholeness or completeness contained within the entire frame or image. A scent is interwoven and "condensed" with memories, associations, feelings, and somatic sensations, which appear to our ego as one "homogeneous" image or smellscape. We would do well to remember this statement from Jung:

> The psyche consists essentially of images. It is a series of images in the truest sense, not an accidental juxtaposition or sequence, but a structure that is throughout full of meaning and purpose; it is a 'picturing' of vital activities. (1928/1969, pp. 325-326)

There are two essential ideas from this passage that I wish to point out. As my research has already demonstrated, our psyche is constantly producing images. But Jung is proposing that, first, these images are not random or chaotic, but rather are structured, and second, that the psychic structure is purposeful. The implication from Jung's assertions is that we must take our images seriously, if for no other reason than they are facts of psychic reality; psychic images exist and present themselves to the ego. Furthermore, not only is our psyche meaningfully structured, but the images themselves may also be meaningful to us. This is important because, "as creatures granted with the gift of reflective consciousness, human beings seek meaning in the depths of space—both inner space as well as outer space" (Coppin & Nelson, 2005, p. 12).

The structure of our psyche may be purposeful, but are all the images in our psyche meaningful? If the answer is no, how do we determine or differentiate which images are meaningful and which are not? To say it differently, how do we assess which of our scent images are full of meaning? What are the qualities or characteristics that make a scent image meaningful? Let us explore the answers to these questions.

Jung might have said the psyche is actually filled with numerous meaningful images, but just how many of those could we say are scent-related or are connected to fragrances in some way? For instance, there is olfactory research that suggests odor-evoked memories are a minority in our psychic universe compared to our other senses: "The occurrence of personally meaningful odor-evoked memories is relatively rare," notes Herz (2016). Other researchers, she adds, "such as Willander and Larsson, suggested that 16% of autobiographical memories are elicited by odors," compared to the other senses, and "by their nature odor-evoked memories involve idiosyncratic experiences" (p. 7). As my research has shown, one of the reasons why scent-evoked memories are so emotionally powerful is because they are relatively uncommon and usually catch us off guard. We don't realize until we smell a particular aroma from our past just how much energy is carried within it and its potential to unleash a multitude of images.

If meaningful scent memories or images are indeed relatively sparse in our psyche compared to our other senses, then it seems to me that due to scarcity their value should therefore be increased. In other words, if we happen to notice a scent memory arise, for instance, it should warrant extra attention simply because it is less common. Are not precious stones, rare books, and exotic perfumes given greater worth partly due to their sparseness? I am not, however, suggesting that simply because a scent memory arises it is automatically deemed meaningful; there are other factors that are involved.

One useful starting point to ascertain whether an image is meaningful or not is our vibrating, pulsing, and sensual soma. To notice how we feel somatically, what our body feels like from the inside, can give us generous and important information. Part of the reflection process is tuning into our somatically felt sense:

> Mirroring is not only reflecting with the mind; it is as well something that happens in the body. It is a presence in posture, a registration in the flesh of events as they take place, those stomach swishes of fear or excitement, the blood draining from hands and feet in coldness, the exhaustion from prolonged tension. In itself this is the sensation

> aspect of mirroring, yet feeling draws values from these reports and makes its judgments. (Hillman, 2013, p. 166)

What happens to us somatically when we reflect on certain scent images? Perhaps we experience a change in our breathing, a tingling of our face, or light-headedness. Or there may be no response or reaction whatsoever, but rather a detached or indifferent feeling when reflection occurs. For instance, the scent of woodchips (as I described above) often elicits a feeling of expansion in my chest, an overall warm sensation in my whole body, as well as mild tightness in my throat. To me these sensations indicate that this particular scent has power, has energy to impress itself upon my soma and psyche. In general, I notice these somatic sensations more easily when I inhale the actual woodchip scent, but I can also contact similar feelings in and through my imagination. In either case, something internal is happening that seems significant; my soma is telling me so. Gendlin (1978) explains one way this process may work:

> One must go to that place where there are not words but only *feeling*. At first there may be nothing there until a felt sense forms. Then when it forms, it feels pregnant. The felt sense has in it a meaning you can feel…when you look for a felt sense, you look in the place you know without words, in body-sensing. (p. 84)

It is the felt sense of "pregnancy" or fullness that I believe is pointing us in the direction of meaningfulness. How do we know a scent image is meaningful? Because we can feel it sensately embodied in our muscles, bones, and viscera.

Tightly bound with our somatic sensations, at times even indistinguishable, are our emotions. Throughout my research I have investigated the critical role that emotions have on the formation of images, memory and to fragrances. When we inhale a scent that stimulates a memory, for instance, the more emotional we feel, the more weight or value we tend to give it. Herz (2016) explains the significance of emotions to meaningful odor-evoked memories:

> Odor-evoked memory or the 'Proust phenomenon'…occurs when an odor triggers the recollection of a meaningful past personal episode…The most distinctive characteristics of odor-evoked memories, however, and why they are important to human health and wellbeing is that they evoke more emotional and evocative recollections than memories triggered by any other cue. (pp. 1-2)

Sadness, disgust, joy, anger, contempt, and fear—any or all of these emotions can be felt when we reflect on a scent image. I contend that since emotion implies value, the stronger the emotion, the more we are pregnant or filled with a sense of importance and meaning. But our emotions are ungrounded and insubstantial without a scent image embedded in or attached to them; the image is a crucial component. "The memory of an experience, the image of the emotions we experience, this is everything, for the image is where the soul resides" (Cowan, 2002, p. 67).

We may feel disgusted, for instance, by the aroma of cottage cheese, but without an image or memory attached to it we may not be able to understand our aversion toward it and therefore it feels less significant. I can imagine, however, that very evocative scents without an image could still feel meaningful simply by the somatic and emotional affects they illicit. Hillman (1979a) elaborates: "We get more sense (significance) from an image the more we note its sense (data), and the more it signifies the more it affects us sensuously, sensately, sensitively" (p. 139). In other words, there is a feedback loop whereby reflection on our emotional scent images leads to deeper meaningfulness, which then leads to more somatic sensations, and so on. The more we pay attention to our scent images, the more we can feel in our body, and the greater our sense of being filled with meaning.

There is yet another way that tells us if a scent image is meaningful—repetition. Sometimes particular scent memories, for instance, capture our attention and we choose to keep the scent and its associations fixed in our awareness. This would typically occur if the images were especially nostalgic—poignant and emotionally powerful. We may recall and experience a scent memory over and over like a powerful song. There is something about it that urges us to ruminate on it and re-experience its essence.

On other occasions images arise, against the will of the ego, for an extended period of time. A scent memory lingers, unwanted, but it will not fade away easily. These are frequently unpleasant images, but important nonetheless. "Repeated remembrance of things past leads to the memorial core of these remembrances, their archetypal meaning and necessity, and to the scintilla of insight in that core" (Hillman, 1972, p. 186). I had one patient who smelled a man in a coffee shop who reminded her of her former husband. This occurred two days before our session and when she arrived it was still fresh in her mind, still clearly bothering her. We took that as an opportunity to discuss some unresolved feelings toward him. She was upset that the scent affected her so much, as well as surprised in her inability to rid the emotions and memories that the scent carried.

As we have touched upon, there is something about repetition and nostalgic reflection that the soul seems to need, similar to a child who wants the same story told numerous times. This is likely due, in part, because stories stimulate the imagination. "Imagining is…a self-regulating act in its own right, with its own type of insight and thus with an intrinsic significance and value" (Casey, 1974b, p. 19). Repetition of scent stories stimulates and regulates the imagination, that great intermediary of the psyche. Or perhaps a scent image repeats itself, or rather we replay it, because there is something important for us to acknowledge and understand about it.

Most of the personal examples I have shared in my research have been scent images that I have often, and intentionally, reflected upon. It is as if my soul needs to go over the same scent memories, relive certain feelings, so that it knows the images intimately, in a heartfelt way. "The sophistication of the heart is its double-beat, an echoing syncopation; or its interior wall, a two-sided mirror by means of which reflective speculations may be taken to heart and imagined further" (Hillman, 2014, p. 56). It is like gazing or staring at someone you love, taking in every feature of their face, noticing the details on their hands and their subtle gestures. If this is the last time we see them we better take in as much as we can, says the soul. Perhaps in a similar way we enter our inner smellscape, each time slightly differently, but with the need to repeat in our imagination particular scent images; and this we ultimately do because we love them:

> Psychological faith begins in the *love of images*, and it flows mainly through the shapes of the persons in reveries, fantasies, reflections, and imaginations. Their increasing vivification gives one an increasing conviction of having, and then of being, an interior reality of deep significance transcending one's personal life. (Hillman, 1975, p. 50)

There is a reason that people instinctively smell their beloved's clothing when they are absent or have died. The fragrance left on the clothing triggers comforting images that are likely quite emotional and undoubtedly evoke numerous memories. Kids as well as adults are known to do this (McBurney, Shoup, & Streeter, 2006) and, like Hillman expressed, this instinctive act enlivens and restores to life an absent person or place. It may even restore us.

Interestingly, there is also research demonstrating the psychological importance of nostalgia, of repetitive reflection on our past images. "There are good reasons to hypothesize that nostalgia is a source of meaning in life…events that encapsulate deep, wholesome, and consequential life experiences—experiences that, when reflected on, may serve to impart a sense of meaning" (Routledge et al., 2011, p. 639). We could go so far as to say that our love of scent images, through repetition, makes us feel that we ourselves are meaningful. When we show our love of particular scent images through repetitive or nostalgic reflection we are engaged in something more than passive reminiscence or dry intellectual analysis of past events. We are engaged with dynamic images that have weight, value, and depth.

But do scent images always remain meaningful to us, or can their sense of weight or value change due to altered perception by the ego? Can they, like fun house mirrors, become distorted or change in a moment in time? Richard Palmer (1969) offers his perspective:

> An event or experience can so alter our lives that what was formerly meaningful becomes meaningless and an apparently unimportant past experience may take on meaning in retrospect. The sense of the whole determines the function and meaning of the parts. And meaning is something historical; it is the relationship of whole to parts seen by us from a given standpoint, at a given time, for a given combination of parts. It is not something above or outside history but a part of a hermeneutical circle always historically defined. (p. 118)

Palmer is making the case that our sense of meaningfulness or meaninglessness can change over time and is therefore not fixed. The fact that meaningfulness can change is important because we tend to think of scent memories and associations as immutable and not subject to alteration. While it is true that once a scent association has formed it is very difficult to modify it, it is also true that our relationship to an aroma can be revised. It is not uncommon to hear of a wife going through a difficult divorce to feel disgusted by her husband's once-adored personal scent. The feeling toward the fragrance likely changed because the emotions and the context changed. Palmer again:

> Meaning and meaningfulness, then, are contextual; they are part of the situation…meaning is historical: it has changed with time; it is a matter of relationship, always related to a perspective from which events are seen. Meaning is not fixed and firm. (pp. 118-119)

Since meaning, according to Palmer, is contextual and historical, we therefore can have a multiplicity of meaning when it comes to scent images. It is like waking up from a dream and realizing after sober reflection that there can certainly be more than one single meaning or interpretation of the dream. "When we realize the inherent multiplicity of meaning in the image itself, we cannot force the dream into any single truth," writes Hillman (1978, p. 156). In the same way, we cannot force a scent image into any one truth. As we grow and change, so too can our relationship to our images and what they mean to us.

During my research I have discovered several meaningful scent images that until recently I had not given much attention to, and consequently did not ever consider to be meaningful. These discoveries have occurred when I have smelled something from my past that I hadn't smelled in a long time. I became awake to their power as I found myself emotionally and somatically stimulated. It also happened when I was engaged in fantasy, pondering over important events of my life and recalling the scents associated with those events. Reflecting on these forgotten or neglected scent images has stirred within me an embodied feeling of meaningfulness.

Freud had a word for this experience of an unexpected surge of meaningfulness: "*"Nachtraglichkeit*: Freud's word, clumsily translated as 'deferred action' or 'belatedness,' which refers to the way historically earlier moments become endowed with originally unsuspected significance and power when evoked, usually unconsciously, by later ones" (Downing, 2006, p. xii). It is as if the earlier moments created an energetic charge and this energy was stored unconsciously until it was activated later.

The point is that what the ego determines to be meaningful can change over time; it is contextual, partially determined by the situation, partly by the relationship between the ego and our scent images. Some meaningful scent images may stay with us for decades and much richness may be gained by reflecting upon them. Other images, once significant, may fade away as if they never existed. Still other scent images may unexpectedly surface with a fullness of meaning, and we may cry or smile as if greeting an old friend.

In closing, I have been interested in personal scent images, or "inner smellscapes," that feel meaningful. I have proposed that the part of the human psyche that determines what images are meaningful is the ego, a mirror-like center of the psyche. Scent images arise in the psyche and the ego may reflect on them.

I have found four ways to determine if scent images are meaningful. First, the information we receive from our somas is an embodied sense of fullness in our muscles, bones, and viscera. We know of meaningfulness directly through the lived experience of our body. Second, we feel strong emotions—the stronger the emotions, the more there is a sense of importance and meaning. Our emotions are a useful clue that our psyche has been provoked. Third, scent images stay with us longer than other images; the aroma and its associations are not easily dismissed. Finally, when we find ourselves engaged in repetitive nostalgic recollection (consciously chosen or not), we can assume that the images are significant enough for our psyche to replay them for some reason or another. Thus, these are the primary ways we can tell if a scent image is meaningful. These ways are, in this sense, our mirrors of meaning.

Since not all the scent images in our psyche are meaningful, we would do well to take the ones that do arise seriously as an act of self-love. It is like looking seriously into a mirror and staring deep into our own eyes. For our meaningful scent images can be powerful in their ability to "reveal a rich mirroring of our inner experience and our interactions with the world outside ourselves" (Downing, 2006, p. 83). In this way we experience the dynamic and rich relationship between aromas and our own soul.

Chapter 6

FINDINGS

Psychological Implications

People say that what we are all seeking
is a meaning for life.
I don't think that's what we're really seeking.
I think what we are seeking
is an experience of being alive.
~Joseph Campbell, *"The Power of Myth"*

A whiff of the universe makes us dream
of worlds we have never seen,
recalls in a flash entire epochs
of our dearest experience.
~Helen Keller, *The World I Live In*

Is not attention always designed for the good or
benefit of that to which the attention is given?
~Socrates

My research has described how an aroma can become a psychic image. It further demonstrated how particular scent images are meaningful to an individual. I have argued that a combination of important factors is involved in this process. These include our imagination, somatic sensations, emotions, memories, and a reflective ego. Where does this leave us, then? In other words, what are the broader psychological implications of my research? Moreover, what is the potential therapeutic value that we may gain from this hermeneutic study?

Before I offer clinical or therapeutic suggestions, let us start with our own psyche, which Jung (1931/1969) says is the "only phenomenon that is given to us immediately and, therefore, is the *sine qua non* of all experience. The only things we experience immediately are the contents of consciousness" (pp. 139-140). So once again we are back to the human psyche, the object that is under investigation as well as the subject doing the inquiry. "The psyche itself then becomes the object of scrutiny and reflection" (Stein, 2015, p. 186).

There must be reasons why we look at ourselves in the mirror, why we turn our gaze inward to self-reflect on our own psychic activity. Hillman (1983b) believes it is because "the soul wants to learn psychology, wants thoughtful formulations of itself, and that this is a mode of its healing" (p. 119). Another idea is offered by Edinger (1992) who writes, "modern man's most urgent need is to discover the reality and value of the inner subjective world of the psyche, to discover the symbolic life" (p. 109). Perhaps we self-reflect so that we know ourselves more deeply, experience self-worth, and to heal.

Yet, asking of the psyche: "how to capture it in our observations? How to relate to it when we do? These are the postmodern issues and questions" (Stein, 2015, p. 186). This kind of subjectivism is considered postmodern because we have turned our attention from the external environment inward to explore our own psychic and somatic landscape. As a new wave of human evolution, the postmodern way leans in the direction of "self-discovery and self-improvement, with the senses and subjective experience acting as the main interface" (Rindisbacher, 2015, p. 75). When it comes more specifically to scents and olfaction, we are aligned on both the postmodern and somatic track. "It can safely be said that the sense of smell has become a guiding modality in postmodern writing. Yet its rise is part of a broader phenomenon: the emergence of the *body* in literature" (Rindisbacher, 2015, p. 83). The first person, subjective experience of the body (somatics) is therefore an appropriate bridge and source of knowledge to understanding our psychic reality.

As my research has shown, fragrances and scent images that induce strong, lasting emotions and memories, affect us somatically, and have a felt sense of meaningfulness, are thought to be significant to the soul. In other words, we are talking about internal experiences that stand out from other events in our life. "The presence of feeling, arousal, and meaning—all indications that eros is stirring—is the hallmark of a soul experience. That is why an experience is always more psychological than a mere event" (Coppin & Nelson, 2005, p. 49). What, then, are the psychological benefits of meaningful scent images?

The first has to do with a feeling of intimacy. As Porteous (1996) points out, "the smells of home, of persons, of pets, of cuddly toys or of a 'security blanket' are reassuring and deepen our sense of attachment to environment and society" (p. 36). Attachment via scent is a type of intimate connection we have with something or someone. Think of the critical bond between mother and baby and the natural body aromas that help maintain this strong, primal connection. One basic human need is for touch and closeness. Recall the importance of scent during the act of kissing, where smelling your partner's face contributes to the feeling of pleasure and intimacy. Pleasure, too, has psychological value. Hillman (1995) elaborates:

> Then there is the power of pleasure. What a dominating hold it has on how we shape our days. I am referring not only to what we eat and what we wear or how we spend our evenings. I mean more the power of colors and tastes, and small talk over our smallest reactions and observations; the power of sensuousness, wit, affection and friendship—the pleasures that move the body and soul and may well be the final goal of all else we do. (pp. 206-207)

A question we can ask ourselves is this: what pleasurable aromas or scent images swoon our soma and enchant our psyche? The answer will lead us in the direction of psychological worth and value.

Testimony from those who have lost their sense of smell show us how vital the experience of olfactory pleasure and intimacy are in a person's life:

> Loss of the sense of smell brings with it severe disruption of mental health and happiness, while smell's intact state brings texture, richness, and a brilliant emotional quality to life in innumerable ways. The emotional enrichment imparted by scent is particularly striking for someone whose life is filled with its pleasures and vividness. (Herz, 2007, p. 16)

I believe Herz is emphasizing the importance of emotional fulfillment that certain scents provide in our life, and the unfortunate consequences arising from their absence. As Bachelard (1942/2006) points out, "we may think that we are being faithful to a favorite image; in reality, we are being faithful to a primitive human feeling" (p. 5). In other words, psychological health is maintained and improved when we experience, via aromas, pleasurable emotional states.

As we have already discussed, emotions are tightly bound with scent memories. "From numerous perspectives it is evident that the autobiographical memories and emotional associations that are triggered by odors are essential to our psychological and physiological health" (Herz, 2016, p. 9). So, we are not only fulfilled emotionally, but we are also fulfilled by particular scent memories. One aspect of memory is that of nostalgia, which is "a sentimental longing for one's valued past, entails bitter-sweet affect, albeit considerably more positive than negative, and refers to momentous occasions where the self and close others come together" (Reid, Green, Wildschut, & Sedikides, 2015, p. 157).

Nostalgia is not simply a desire to return to our past, but rather it is an imaginative engagement with a meaningful and valued past. "Nostalgia is a psychological resource that can be harnessed to derive and sustain a sense of meaning in life" (Routledge et al., 2011, p. 647). Further, as we have all come to know over time, "perceiving one's life as full of meaning and purpose is a hallmark of healthy psychological functioning" (Routledge et al., 2011, p. 638). One aspect of life that humans seem unable to live without is meaning and purpose. Thus, most researchers agree on the importance of nostalgia for psychological health, but until recently few have suggested or encouraged the use of aromas to elicit such effects. Herz (2016) summarizes this idea well:

> Beyond the specificity of memory, nostalgia—reflecting upon one's personal past—has been shown to have many beneficial psychological consequences. Engaging in nostalgic reminiscence increases positive affect, bolsters self-esteem, strengthens the connection between one's past and present, produces feelings of social connectedness, elevates optimism, and infuses life with meaning. Recent research suggests that odor-evoked memories may be especially nostalgic triggers. (p. 4)

In other words, it is psychologically and physiologically healthy to engage in nostalgic reflection on scent memories. Perhaps the greatest benefit from this is the engendering of meaningfulness in one's life.

Meaningful scent images also play a role in our identity, possibly influencing the formation and maintenance of who we think we are. Let us remember the power that personal images have on our psyche. "Living images are highly idiosyncratic and psychoactive, meaning that they stimulate distinct physical and emotional responses" (Coppin & Nelson, 2005, p. 64). This is certainly the case for scent images. For example, even if the fragrance of vanilla is experienced as pleasurable to many people, each person will have their own particular memories and associations—their own inner smellscape—that will make their scent image distinct. We cannot forget this fact because, as Lockhart (1987) observes, "what gets overlooked and quickly forgotten is the fine and subtle detail that is unique—

absolutely unique. Yet one's exact fate and individuality are tied to those details" (p. 54).

The idiosyncratic details of our scent images may therefore play a part in our sense of self. We see this phenomenon at work in our perception and memory of others. After a close friend or pet has died, for instance, what about them do we remember? It is usually not general characteristics but rather the specific and particular—a strange habit, a favorite corner of the room where they slept, the way they chopped vegetables, or the sound of their sneeze. In a similar way, our own personal images build and support our character, giving us a reference point from which to know ourselves. As Woodman (1993) stresses, "you have to follow your own images. It's the only way to find out who you are" (p. 94).

It is my belief that meaningful images are important in discovering who we are. I am speaking here of those scent images that are reflected to our ego as revealing and indicative of our dearest experiences. "By virtue of having an ego—this built in mirror within consciousness—we can know that we are and what we are" (Stein, 2015, p. 22). Insofar as scent images or memories stay with us for many years, not easily forgotten or dismissed, we may deem them significant to our sense of self.

It is as if our inner smellscape provides a refuge, a familiar psychic space that we can enter so as to reconnect with parts of our self. Trust and faith in our own images ground us in our self. "Psychological faith is reflected in an ego that gives credit to images and turns to them in its darkness. Its trust is in the imagination as the only incontrovertible reality, directly presented, immediately felt" (Hillman, 1975, p. 50). Our conviction that meaningful scent images reflect who we are is confirmed through our emotional soma and fertile imagination.

I am aware that the notion of identity and how it is formed and preserved is complex, comprised of many facets, and not without controversy. I simply want to propose that one of the functions and benefits of scent images is to contribute to our sense of self. Downing (2006) puts it like this:

> Our lives are shaped by our thoughts and deeds and, even more powerfully, our fantasies and dreams, and the complex feeling-toned associations with which we respond to the persons and events we encounter daily. I am not merely what I have thought, as Descartes proposed, nor simply what I have done, as the existentialists claim, but also, as Gaston Bachelard has so powerfully shown, what I have imagined and remembered. (pp. 84-85)

Our fantasies, memories, and psychic images are indeed powerful. A meaningful scent image of a loved one can bring us to tears or fill us with nostalgia for a place long ago abandoned. These images can come unexpectedly, often to the surprise and dismay of our ego. Whether we are irritated, amused, or comforted by our scent images, at least we know that we exist.

Thus, reflection on meaningful aromas leads to a kind of self-knowledge. As Ricoeur puts it, "any increment in knowledge results from an interaction of the imagination with reflective and critical modes of knowing, prior to any final incorporation into our present worldview" (as cited in Eliade, 1987, p. 108). In other words, it is the relationship between the ego and meaningful images in the psyche that helps us understand and know who and what we are. There is psychological value inherent in this form of knowing.

An objection could be raised that a scent image has no objective reality and therefore cannot be a valid form of knowledge. While subjective images may not be physically real, they are, however, psychically real. Jung (1923/1971) explains:

> Although, as a rule, no reality-value attaches to the image, this can at times actually increase its importance for psychic life, since it then has a greater *psychological* value, representing an inner reality which often far outweighs the importance of external reality. (p. 442)

This statement by Jung is especially important, I believe, because our culture today tends to place greater emphasis and value on external, "objective" reality over our psychic life.

Yet by observing our psychic landscape we not only know ourselves more deeply, we also know the world and its features more intimately. Ultimately, I see this as an act of love. "Attention is paid, credit given, not for the sake of consciousness, the duty of analysis, but because you take delight in watching the behavior of psychic processes, the enjoyment of recognitions and insights as things disclose themselves" (Hillman, 1978, p. 181). It is like watching our own facial expressions in a mirror, surprised and awed at both their beauty and strangeness.

To gain the most from our meaningful scent images we must be attuned to a certain psychological wavelength that collaborates with our beautiful, animal-sensing body. "When we walk through the world aesthetically," observes Hillman (1979a), "then we experience images like breath through the nostrils, a reflex consciousness on which life depends…This *via aesthetica* would be what is meant by 'living psychologically'" (pp. 142-143). Moreover, to live psychologically is to also be acutely aware of our pulsing and throbbing body, our somatic felt sense. Let us recall that our olfactory sense is one of the oldest and most primal. It is not impossible to conceive that we have been making and living scent images for thousands of years. As Hillman (1983a) reminds us:

> We are sensuously imagining animals. The first thing the psyche does is make sensuous images. So why not imagine a psychology that starts there, in the aesthetic nature of human being and the aesthetic nature of the world which displays itself in sense events, to the senses, and the first reaction is to live a thing as a sense image. Things have skins and faces and smells. (pp. 144-145)

We see once again that there is a relationship or interaction between the human psyche and soma and the constantly changing world of objects as they generously present themselves.

What purpose does this relationship serve? Let us explore briefly one last psychological implication, one that deals with our collective human potential toward the evolution of consciousness itself.

The idea of expanding or deepening of consciousness proposes that along with the evolution of the planet, species are co-evolving, including humans. One aspect of this evolution is that of human consciousness. It may not be enough for our species to simply live our life as we desire, nor merely to survive. Perhaps we are to become more conscious, more aware, so that we may reflect the cosmos back to itself. In fact, this was one of Jung's ideas. Stein (2015) explains:

> He [Jung] saw the meaning of human life on this planet to be tied to our capacity for consciousness, to add to the world a mirroring awareness of things and meanings that otherwise would run on through endless eons of time without being seen, thought, or recognized. (p. 214)

Since aromas are part of the world, our attention to, experience of, and thoughts about them would contribute to the conscious unfolding of the cosmos itself. Humans, Jung believes, "have a special role to play in the universe. Our consciousness is capable of reflecting the cosmos and bringing it into the mirror of consciousness" (as cited in Stein, 2015, p. 220). To a certain degree our inner smellscape mirrors the outer smellscape, and it is through this dialectical relationship that the cosmos comes to know itself. Or as Stein writes, "the individual is a co-creator of the reflection of reality that history as a whole reveals" (2015, p. 216).

That odors and our personal scent images have a role to play in the evolution of consciousness may be amusing to some people and absurd to others. After all, "compared to the intricately detailed scenes presented by visual experiences especially, olfactory experiences are mere smudges on our consciousness" (Batty, 2010, p. 518). While it is true that vision and audition dominate our sensory experience, we must not minimize the significance olfaction has on both our lives and the expanding universe. Scent experiences are "mere smudges" only when we fail to notice and give value to the power aromas have on consciousness.

By valorizing our internal smellscape, we likewise honor and validate the world of aromas. As Hillman (1972) expresses elegantly, "by being touched, moved, and opened by the experience of the soul, one discovers that what goes on in the soul is not only interesting and meaningful, necessary and acceptable, but that it is attractive, lovable, and beautiful" (pp. 101-102). The immense variety of aromas in our environment does indeed have an effect on our consciousness as well as our soul. By being altered, we co-creators give back to the cosmos our scent experiences, our memories, and our images.

In sum, I have outlined several psychological benefits of meaningful scent images. My research showed that these images induce a feeling of intimacy and attachment between someone and something. Meaningful scents provide emotional fulfillment, while nostalgic and memorial activities lead to another kind of fulfillment. Meaningful aromas engender an overall feeling of meaning and purpose, which are components of psychological health. Other benefits include an increase in self-esteem, self-worth, and a strengthening of the sense of life continuity. My research also demonstrated that meaningful scent images are involved in the formation and preservation of one's identity and greater self-knowledge. Finally, through reflection on our significant scent images we gain knowledge of the olfactory world as well as discover our unique role in the evolution of consciousness itself.

Clinical and Therapeutic Implications

As some researchers have pointed out, "the sense of smell and the memories it brings have rarely been part of the therapeutic interaction, even though studies on odors and memory were done as early as 1935" (La Torre, 2003, p. 35). There are, however, therapeutic benefits in engaging with meaningful memories, images, and feelings related to scents. How can we take our knowledge of olfaction and our understanding of meaningful scent images and offer it to those in the helping professions? From private psychotherapy offices, to rehabilitation centers, to public health clinics, the range of potential application of this research is wide. In this section I will present two concrete examples of how this research might be implemented. It is my hope that clinicians, doctors, nurses, and therapists will be able to take practical value from this research and apply it in their own work.

Let me give a potential scenario from the perspective of a psychotherapist. A woman in her mid-fifties comes into therapy after experiencing an auto accident three months prior. She reports that since the accident she has suffered from neck pain and migraines, which have affected her work. She explains that her sleep has been poor due to the physical pain and from disturbing dreams. After talking to the therapist further, she reveals that she has been experiencing memory problems, both short-term and long-term. Her bad memory causes her great upset, which has led to feelings of anxiety, frustration, and depression. She feels too young to have such cognitive impairments. In the worst of these moments she experiences panic attacks. She admits that for most of her life she has rarely felt safe in the world, and since the accident she feels even less safe.

Let us now look at how the psychotherapist in our example could incorporate fragrances and scent images into the therapeutic relationship. A starting point for the therapist may be to ask the client to recall a time in her life that she felt the most safe. The therapist could encourage the client to flush out as many details of this past moment of safety, including what scents were present at the time. In this way the client may become aware of a connection to an aroma that has an association of safety. If possible, the client is encouraged to first find, and then inhale, her "safety scent" when she feels anxious, afraid, or unsafe. It is not impossible that inhaling her safety scent may also help her neck pain and migraines. These suggestions are supported by olfactory research. Herz (2016) explains:

> When odors are capable of eliciting emotional and physical changes it is due to the emotions, memories and associations that have been linked to an odor through past personal experiences, which are then elicited when the odor is encountered, and the psychological and physiological responses connected to the odor are recapitulated. It is this way that odor-evoked memories have been empirically verified to alter emotional, mental and physical states and thus how they may be used in therapeutic applications. (p. 9)

In terms of the client's memory problems, the therapist might use the olfactory sense as a way to bring confidence to the client by strengthening her long-term memory. The therapist could ask, for instance, about a happy memory from childhood and any associated scents from that time in her life. As researchers have noted, "just talking about a scent can bring a whole host of memories into the interaction. Studies have shown that thinking about the scent can be as powerful as the scent itself" (La Torre, 2003, p. 35). If the scent is potent enough, it could be a strong catalyst for other memories and associations that she has difficulty remembering.

For help with short-term memory, the therapist could offer an unfamiliar essential oil, for example, that the client enjoys, and have her carry it in her purse or car and inhale the oil when she needs to mentally record something important. In this way, the novel scent is connected to an important item that needs to be recalled. There is research to support the idea that fragrances can be used to enhance memory by a well-established psychological phenomenon called context-dependent memory. "When you are in the same context, place, or mind-set that you were in when you learned something, you remember that information better" (Herz, 2007, p. 80). Helping her memory may therefore alleviate some of her feelings of anxiety and frustration associated with her poor memory.

Another way to improve the client's memory is to engage her imagination. Since imagination plays a role in creating and retrieving memories, therapists can help their clients by stimulating their memory and imagination through the use of scent. One method the therapist could employ is to introduce an assortment of common essential oils for their client to smell. If there is a strong emotional reaction to any of the scents, that aroma could be a starting point to explore the associations and memories that are constellated.

In my own medical clinic, where I practice Chinese medicine, I keep a variety of oils for my patients to inhale and sometimes place on their body. It is remarkable what happens to them when we find a scent they greatly enjoy. I often observe a deepening of their breathing and a marked relaxation of their shoulders and face. As Herz (2007) notes, "an odor you enjoy will make you feel good and can decrease your anxiety and increase your tolerance to environmental annoyances" (p. 97).

Sometimes, however, the essential oil fragrance is quite disagreeable. Such an unpleasant aroma may also have associations and memories worth investigating. If the client feels safe in the therapeutic relationship, this might be a time for the therapist to consider deeper work with their imagination. One method, known as *active imagination*, is a prime example where the sense of smell can be included in the therapy.

During active imagination, the client would explore and engage with their psychic images. If, for instance, vivid memories of Christmas surface when the client inhales peppermint essential oil, the therapist could encourage the client to "return to Christmas" in her imagination and recall as many details as possible. She could also interact with people or animals from the Christmas memory, which could give her a sense of security. The point here is, "in attending to the soul's deepest need, the essential question is not so much *what* I remember, but *how* I remember it" (Cowan, 2002, p. 60). The "how" of remembering is pointing to the specifics of the memory, and the way our imagination forms and deforms images.

Finally, to help with the client's disturbing dreams, active imagination could also be employed. In this case, the client returns to a past dream, or part of a dream, and interacts with whatever or whomever is there. After dialoging it is often discovered that what was frightful or grotesque in the dream turns out to be benign or helpful. The exploration of any scents in the dream might be worth inquiring. I must point out that active imagination can involve much more than what I described, but for my purposes here I simply want to present a basic example.

Thus, through the method of active imagination, not only can the client's memory be stimulated, but she can also discover parts of her psyche she did not know existed, thereby deepening self-understanding. This occurs through slow and patient inquiry of a single scent image and will sometimes reveal meaning and insight that was not at first apparent:

> If an image does not have to refer beyond itself to gain significance, neither does our therapy that works with and from images. Soul-making needs no external referent. The activity of therapy receives its meaning and value from the activity itself. (Hillman, 1978, p. 176)

It is in these ways the psychotherapist could incorporate fragrances and scent images into the therapeutic relationship.

Let us look at another example to see how we may apply my research. At a rehab clinic for drug addiction, one therapist is working with a 22-year-old boy who has been addicted to methamphetamines for over a year. As a college student he had difficulty focusing while studying and taking tests and turned to drugs to help him concentrate. The client expressed that he has been physically and emotionally exhausted due to overstimulation from both the drugs and life in general. The therapist notes that he frequently dissociates; he has trouble bringing awareness to parts of his body as well as his emotions. He also suffers from low self-esteem, loneliness, and a lack of meaning in his life.

Let us look at how the therapist in our example can include fragrances and scent images in their clinical work. At some point in the recovery from drug addiction it is necessary for the client to return to their body and their emotions, both of which have typically been numb or disowned. The use of fragrances and odor-evoked memories may help in this regard. The therapist could use essential oils or some other fragrant object as a starting point. The therapist himself could inhale, let's say, lime essential oil and then share whatever the scent stimulates. The therapist can demonstrate: "Ahhh, whenever I smell lime it always takes me back to partying in Mexico when I was in college. I felt so free during those days." After a moment of reflection, the therapist can ask the client, "Do you enjoy the smell of lime? Would you like to smell it?" Opening a casual conversation around scents can be a gentle way to help the client tune into their body and emotions. Observe the following research findings:

> Mentioning certain scents or asking about odors during a session can bring about a deeper discussion of feelings and emotions, allowing the client to tune into the experience more intimately,

to feel it more directly, and to connect with it on a fuller level. (La Torre, 2003, p. 35)

Insofar as feelings are a primary focal point in many kinds of therapy, it makes sense to include odors and their associated emotions in the therapeutic exchange. One of the advantages of using aromas to connect with emotions is that they often lead to the sharing of personal stories. To create the space for the client to simply tell stories from their life may be healing for them in and of itself. As Hillman (1975) expresses:

> We are different at the end of the story because the soul has gone through a process during the telling, independent of its syntax and full understanding of its words…Through the telling of events—which is what *mythos* originally meant—the soul takes random images and happenings and makes them into particular lived experiences…Psychological living implies living in a fantasy, a story, being told by a myth. (p. 143)

A personal story told to the therapist may have an aroma or two as the thrust of the narrative, or it may just be a tangential detail that adds nuance and texture to the client's tale. In either case the client, by connecting with his scent memories, may edge back into his body and feel his emotions.

Furthermore, the therapist could encourage a deeper exploration of a happy scent memory in which the client felt connected to other people, places, or animals. This may help with his feelings of loneliness and low self-esteem. Herz (2016) explains: "Any odor that for a given individual evokes a happy autobiographical memory has the potential to increase positive emotions, decrease negative moods, disrupt cravings, lower stress and increase physiological wellbeing" (p. 9). Beyond the work done in the therapeutic setting, the client would also benefit from actually wearing a scent that induces uplifting emotions. This would allow the client to remain in contact with the scent memories throughout the day, providing a valuable therapeutic resource.

If I were the therapist I would bring my box of essential oils and let him smell them all until we find one he really likes. There are numerous essential oils that help calm the nervous system (rose geranium, for instance), and therefore be useful to alleviate his feeling of overstimulation. In this way his choice of fragrant oil would be used as a starting point to open a conversation, as well as a source of comfort.

As we have discovered from olfactory research, our scent associations are often formed early in life and hold fast for many years and are unlikely to change or disappear. There is a therapeutic advantage for an odor association to resist change: "The special resistance to retroactive interference that is fundamental to olfactory cognition can make a specific odor linked to a meaningful past personal event extremely reliable as a therapeutic agent" (Herz, 2016, p. 9). This insight has practical therapeutic value in our example. The young man, like many other Americans, lacks meaning in his life. As Edinger (1992) points out, "one of the symptoms of alienation in the modern age is the widespread sense of meaninglessness…there is increasing evidence of a general psychic disorientation. We have lost our bearings. Our relation to life has become ambiguous" (p. 107). Reminding the young man that scents can be meaningful, or are part of a meaningful experience, may help with "psychic disorientation." A deeper exploration of his meaningful scent images might prove to be an effective adjunct treatment in his recovery from addiction.

To conclude this section and to bring together the ideas expressed in it, let us be willing to see the therapeutic versatility of working with aromas and meaningful scent images. The examples presented are intended to demonstrate ways this research may be applied in different clinical situations. It is my hope that readers will take the basic ideas from this research and apply it where they see fit.

Conclusion

In contrast to the wide range of scientific research in vision and audition, olfaction has historically been given less attention. This is as true in the natural sciences as it is in the field of depth psychology. A review of the literature in depth psychology has revealed a gap in the subject of olfaction. Nevertheless, in recent decades there has been a surge of olfactory research that has investigated the importance of odors for physical and psychological health, especially on the topics of emotion and memory. However, the idea that scent can be a meaningful psychic image is seldom discussed, even in the field of depth psychology.

The research presented here examined the hypothesis that a scent can be a psychic image and the factors that give rise to meaningful scent images and the implications they have for the human soul. A hermeneutic methodology was employed to answer these questions.

Texts from depth psychology, philosophy, and the natural sciences were used to inform one another and synthesize relevant ideas. The results have shown that a scent can indeed be a psychic image. I identified several important qualities that are involved in the formation of scent images. First, an odor is linked to a particular evocative and emotional experience. The context of the experience involves idiosyncratic details including strong somatic sensations. This creates a psychic memory image that sticks and is not easily forgotten. These images may range from extremely beautiful to outright disgusting.

However, I suggested that memory is a phenomenon of "a" reality, not the only reality. I argued that the ego is in close relationship with the imagination, an intermediate imaginal realm where fantasy activity colors and textures all psychic experiences. I therefore proposed that we conceptualize scent images as existing within an "inner smellscape," where our scent memories and associations intersect with our imagination. Moreover, we may reflect upon our inner smellscape for the purpose of understanding ourselves more deeply.

My research has also shown that some scent images possess more weight than others and are therefore more meaningful to an individual. I proposed that we know a scent image is meaningful if it is highly emotional, somatically activating, and carries a sense of fullness and value. These powerful images often impress us beyond the will or control of our ego and tend to leave a lasting mark on our soul.

Insofar as the human psyche knows itself through its interaction with the environment, we must include olfaction in our discourse. Odorants and their effect upon our soma and psyche need to be considered more precisely and with finer care. We can accomplish this by attuning to the subtleties of our somatic and psychic experiences. Therefore, a depth psychological approach to olfaction can contribute to the field by adding a different perspective to olfactory experience. As Moore (1989) points out, "Hillman recommends that we take an olfactory approach to images, knowing them with the intimacy of smell" (p. 51). I want to twist his idea and encourage others to take an imagistic approach to smells, to know them with the intimacy of image. I am hopeful that my research will call attention to scents and the olfactory experience within the field of depth psychology.

Future Directions

One area that future research might examine is the conceptual framework that I have put forth, for my research did not attempt to test this framework in the field. Rather, the focus was a review and synthesis of the literature and did not involve primary research. I believe the conceptual framework that I presented could be tested in a variety of contexts, and certainly could be best tested in a therapeutic setting.

The methodology employed in my research is hermeneutics and thus does not deal directly with human subjects. While interpretation and analysis of texts lead to new insights, it would be fruitful to conduct research with humans and empirical facts using this conceptual framework. One such quantitative study could investigate the role that meaningful scent images have on human behavior.

A finding that I did not anticipate was the important role the human soma has in revealing whether an aroma or a scent image is meaningful. The stimulation of the physical body proved to be an essential factor in this regard, and future research could give more attention to the lived experience of the body.

A challenge for future research would be to look at scent images from a developmental perspective. Can meaningful scent images change over time, and if so, how? Are there differences between a child's experience of scent images and that of an elderly person? What kind of methodologies could be used to conduct this research?

It would also be worth investigating the idea that scent images can be "inherited," in other words, are non-personal, primordial, or ancestral. This idea might augment the premise of my research that meaningful scent images are inherently personal and are created by experiences in the present life. How are odors and scent images experienced by the collective unconscious? Can one person share very similar scent memories and associations with the same scent? When a group of people experience a scent at the same time, what are the similarities and differences in their psychic experience? Do individuals experience common scents in their nightly dreams, and if so, what might this tell us about the human psyche?

A final challenge would be to probe deeper into the use of language and survey the diverse ways humans have of describing their inner smellscapes and meaningful scent images. For example, one recent study of French and Canadian adults, found that culture and the availability of semantic information had significant effects on olfactory perception at both the verbal and non-verbal levels (Ferdenzi et al., 2017). Since the context of my research was based in American culture and utilized the English language, future research could look at how other cultures describe their scent experiences from the standpoint of their native language.

REFERENCES

Abram, D. (1996). *The spell of the sensuous*. New York, NY: Vintage Books.

Ackerman, D. (1990). *The natural history of the senses*. New York, NY: Random House.

Altundag, A., Salihoglu, M., Cayonu, M., Cingi, C., Tekeli, H., & Hummel, T. (2014). The effect of high altitude on olfactory functions. *European Archives of Oto-Rhino-Laryngology*, 271(3), 615-618.

Auden, W. H. (1962). *The dyer's hand and other essays*. New York, NY: Random House.

Bachelard, G. (1969). *The poetics of reverie* (D. Russell, Trans.). Boston, MA: Beacon Press. (Original work published 1960)

Bachelard, G. (1988). *Air and dreams* (E. C. Farrell, Trans.). Dallas, TX: The Dallas Institute Publications. (Original work published 1943)

Bachelard, G. (1994). *The poetics of space* (M. Jolas, Trans.). Boston, MA: Beacon Press. (Original work published 1958)

Bachelard, G. (2006). *Water and dreams: An essay on the imagination of matter*. Dallas, TX: Dallas Institute of Humanities and Culture. (Original work published 1942)

Batty, C. (2010). A representational account of olfactory experience. *Canadian Journal of Philosophy*, 40(4), 511–538.

Berry, P. (2008). *Echo's subtle body: Contributions to an archetypal psychology*. Putnam, CT: Spring Publications.

Bettelheim, B. (1982). *Freud and man's soul*. New York, NY: Alfred A. Knoph.

Campbell, J. (1986). *The inner reaches of outer space: Metaphor as myth and as religion*. Novato, CA: New World Library.

Casey, E. S. (1974a). Toward an archetypal imagination. *Spring Publications*, 1–25.

Casey, E. S. (1974b). Toward a phenomenology of imagination. *Journal of the British Society for Phenomenology*, 5(1), 3–19.

Coppin, J., & Nelson, E. (2005). *The art of inquiry: A depth psychological perspective*. New York, NY: Spring Publications.

Corbin, H. (1972). Mundus imaginalis or the imaginary and the imaginal. *Spring Publications*, 1–13.

Cowan, L. (2002). *Tracking the white rabbit: A subversive view of modern culture*. New York, NY: Brunner-Routledge.

Delplanque, S., Chrea, C., Grandjean, D., Ferdenzi, C., Cayeux, I., Porcherot, C., Calve, B., Sander, D., & Scherer, K. (2012). How to map the affective semantic space of scents. *Cognition and Emotion, 26*(5), 885–898.

Downing, C. (2006). *Gleanings: Essays 1982–2006*. New York, NY: iUniverse.

Edinger, E. F. (1992). *Ego and archetype: Individuation and the religious function of the psyche*. Boston, MA: Shambhala.

Edinger, E. F. (1994). *Anatomy of the psyche*. Chicago, IL: Open Court Publishing.

Ekman, P. (2003). *Emotions revealed: Recognizing faces and feelings to improve communication and emotional life*. New York, NY: St. Martin's Griffin.

Eliade, M. (1987). *The encyclopedia of religion* (Vol. 7, pp. 104–114). New York, NY: Macmillan.

Ellenberger, H. (1970). *The discovery of the unconscious: The history and evolution of dynamic psychiatry*. New York, NY: Basic Books.

Engen, T. (1982). *The perception of odors*. New York, NY: Academic Press.

Engen, T. (1991). *Odor sensation and memory*. New York, NY: Praeger Publishers.

Ferdenzi, C., Joussain, P., Digard, B., Luneau, L., Djordjevic, J., & Bensafi, M. (2017). Individual differences in verbal and non-verbal affective responses to smells: Influence of odor label across cultures. *Chemical Senses, 42*(1), 37–46.

Freud, S. (2010). *Civilization and its discontents* (J. Riviere, Trans.). New York, NY: W. W. Norton. (Original work published 1930)

Gadamer, H. G. (2006). *Truth and method* (2nd ed., J. Weinsheimer & D. Marshall, Trans.). London, England: Continuum Publishing Group. (Original work published 1975)

Geldard, R. G. (2000). *Remembering Heraclitus*. Great Barrington, MA: Lindisfarne Books.

Gendlin, E. (1978). *Focusing*. New York, NY: Everest House Publishers.

Gilbert, A. (2008). *What the nose knows*. New York, NY: Crown Publishers.

Grondin, J. (1994). *Introduction to philosophical hermeneutics*. New Haven, CT: Yale University Press.

Guerer, A. L. (1992). *Scent: The mysterious and essential powers of smell*. New York, NY: Random House.

Hanna, T. (1970). *Bodies in revolt*. New York, NY: Holt, Rinehart, & Winston.

Hanna, T. (1995). What is somatics? In H. Johnson (Ed.), *Bone, breath, and gesture: Practices of embodiment* (pp. 341–352). Berkeley, CA: North Atlantic Books.

Herz, R. (2007). *The scent of desire: Discovering our enigmatic sense of smell*. New York, NY: HarperCollins Publishers.

Herz, R. (2009). Aromatherapy facts and fictions: A scientific analysis of olfactory effects on mood, physiology, and behavior. *International Journal of Neuroscience, 119*, 263–290.

Herz, R. (2016). The role of odor-evoked memory in psychological and physiological health. *Brain Sciences, 6*, 22, 1–13.

Hillman, J. (1960). *Emotion: A comprehensive phenomenology of theories and their meanings for therapy*. Evanston, IL: Northwestern University Press.

Hillman, J. (1972). *The myth of analysis*. Evanston, IL: Northwestern University Press.

Hillman, J. (1975). *Re-visioning psychology*. New York, NY: Harper and Row.

Hillman, J. (1977). An inquiry into image. *Spring Publications,* 62–88.

Hillman, J. (1978). Further notes on images. *Spring Publications*, 171–185.

Hillman, J. (1979a). Image sense. *Spring Publications,* 152–182.

Hillman, J. (1979b). *The dream and the underworld*. New York, NY: Harper and Row.

Hillman, J. (1983a). *Inter views*. Dallas, TX: Spring Publications.

Hillman, J. (1983b). *Healing fiction*. Putnam, CT: Spring Publications.

Hillman, J. (1995). *Kinds of power*. New York, NY: Doubleday.

Hillman, J. (1999). *The force of character*. New York, NY: Random House.

Hillman, J. (2014). *The thought of the heart and the soul of the world*. Putnam, CT: Spring Publications.

Hillman, J. (2016a). Landscape: A psychological inquiry. In E. Casey (Ed.), *Philosophical intimations: Uniform edition* (Vol. 8, pp. 359–369). Thompson, CT: Spring Publications.

Hillman, J. (2016b). Three conversations with Edward S. Casey. In E. Casey (Ed.), *Philosophical intimations: Uniform edition* (Vol. 8, pp. 407–425). Thompson, CT: Spring Publications.

Hillman, J. (2016c). About epistrophe and therapy: Some notes. In E. Casey (Ed.), *Philosophical intimations: Uniform edition* (Vol. 8, pp. 245–247). Thompson, CT: Spring Publications.

Hillman, J. (2016d). You taught me language. In E. Casey (Ed.), *Philosophical intimations: Uniform edition*

236

(Vol. 8, pp. 40–54). Thompson, CT: Spring
Publications.

Hillman, J. (2016e). Beauty and war: An exploration. In E.
Casey (Ed.), *Philosophical intimations: Uniform
edition* (Vol. 8, pp. 315–330). Thompson, CT:
Spring Publications.

Hillman, J. (2016f). Talking as walking. In E. Casey (Ed.),
Philosophical intimations: Uniform edition (Vol.
8, pp. 37–39). Thompson, CT: Spring Publications.

Hillman, J., & von Franz, M. L. (2013). The feeling
function. *Lectures on Jung's typology* (pp. 166).
Putnam, CT: Spring Publications.

Huysmans, J. K., (2002). *The damned [La-bas]*. London,
England: Penguin Books.

Jung, C. G. (1959). The ego (R. F. C. Hull, Trans.). In H.
Read et al. (Series Eds.), *The collected works of C.
G. Jung* (Vol. 9, pt. 2, pp. 3–7). Princeton, NJ:
Princeton University Press. (Original work
published 1951)

Jung, C. G. (1960). The feeling-toned complex and its
general effects on the psyche (R. F. C. Hull,
Trans.). In H. Read et al. (Series Eds.), *The
collected works of C. G. Jung* (Vol. 3, pp. 3–7).
Princeton, NJ: Princeton University Press.
(Original work published 1909)

Jung, C. G. (1969a). Basic postulates of analytical
psychology (R. F. C. Hull, Trans.). In H. Read et
al. (Series Eds.), *The collected works of C. G. Jung*
(Vol. 8, 2nd ed., pp. 338–357). Princeton, NJ:
Princeton University Press. (Original work
published 1933)

Jung, C. G. (1969). Consciousness, unconsciousness, and individuation (R. F. C. Hull, Trans.). In H. Read et al. (Series Eds.), *The collected works of C. G. Jung* (Vol. 9 pt. 1, 2nd ed., pp. 275–289). Princeton, NJ: Princeton University Press. (Original work published 1939)

Jung, C. G. (1969). On the nature of the psyche (R. F. C. Hull, Trans.). In H. Read et al. (Series Eds.), *The collected works of C. G. Jung* (Vol. 8, 2nd ed., pp. 160–234). Princeton, NJ: Princeton University Press. (Original work published 1954)

Jung, C. G. (1969). Spirit and life (R. F. C. Hull, Trans.). In H. Read et al. (Series Eds.), *The collected works of C. G. Jung* (Vol. 8, 2nd ed., pp. 319-337). Princeton, NJ: Princeton University Press. (Original work published 1928)

Jung, C. G. (1969b). The real and the surreal (R. F. C. Hull, Trans.). In H. Read et al. (Series Eds.), *The collected works of C. G. Jung* (Vol. 8, 2nd ed., p. 384). Princeton, NJ: Princeton University Press. (Original work published 1933)

Jung, C. G. (1969). The structure of the psyche (R. F. C. Hull, Trans.). In H. Read et al. (Series Eds.), *The collected works of C. G. Jung* (Vol. 8, 2nd ed., pp. 139–158). Princeton, NJ: Princeton University Press. (Original work published 1931)

Jung, C. G. (1970). Cryptomnesia (R. F. C. Hull, Trans.). In H. Read et al. (Series Eds.), *The collected works of C. G. Jung* (Vol. 1, 2nd ed., pp. 95–109). Princeton, NJ: Princeton University Press. (Original work published 1905)

Jung, C. G. (1971). Psychological types (R. F. C. Hull, Trans.). In H. Read et al. (Series Eds.), *The collected works of C.G. Jung* (Vol. 6, 3rd ed., pp. 85–486). Princeton, NJ: Princeton University Press. (Original work published 1923)

Jung, C. G. (1976). Symbols and the interpretation of dreams (R. F. C. Hull, Trans.). In H. Read et al. (Series Eds.), *The collected works of C.G. Jung* (Vol. 18, 2nd ed., pp. 183-264). Princeton, NJ: Princeton University Press. (Original work published 1961)

Keller, H. (2009). *The world I live in & optimism: A collection of essays.* Mineola, NY: Dover Publications.

Keller, H., Sullivan, A., Macy, J. A., Shattuck, R., & Herrmann, D. (2003). *The story of my life: The restored classic 1903–2003.* New York, NY: Norton.

La Torre, M. A. (2003). Aromatherapy and the use of scents in psychotherapy. *Perspectives in Psychiatric Care, 39*(1), 35–37.

Lakoff, G., & Johnson, M. (1980). *Metaphors we live by.* Chicago, IL: University of Chicago Press.

Lakoff, G., & Johnson, M. (1999). *Philosophy in the flesh: The embodied mind and its challenge to Western thought.* New York, NY: Basic Books.

Larsson, M., Willander, J., Karlsson, K., & Arshamian, A. (2014). Olfactory LOVER: Behavioral and neural correlates of autobiographical odor memory. *Frontiers in Psychology, 5*(312), 1–5.

Lawrence, D. H. (1959). *Sex, literature, and censorship.* New York, NY: The Viking Press.

Lawrence, D. H. (1961). *Studies in classic American literature*. New York, NY: The Viking Press.

Lawrence, D. H. (1965). *Four short novels*. New York, NY: The Viking Press.

Lawrence, D. H. (1977). *The portable D. H. Lawrence* (D. Trilling, Ed.). New York, NY: Penguin Books.

Lawrence, D. H. (2009). *Mornings in Mexico*. New York, NY: Tauris Parke Paperbacks.

Leaver, R. (2008). The work of James Hillman: City and soul, and Providence, RI. In S. Marlan (Ed.), *Archetypal psychologies: Reflections in honor of James Hillman* (pp. 439–460). New Orleans, LA: Spring Journal Books.

Lockhart, R. (1987). *Psyche speaks: A Jungian approach to self and world*. Wilmette, IL: Chiron Publications.

McBurney, D. H., Shoup, M. L., & Streeter, S. A. (2006). Olfactory comfort: Smelling a partner's clothing during periods of separation. *Journal of Applied Social Psychology, 36*(9), 2325–2335.

Merleau-Ponty, M. (2012). *Phenomenology of perception* (D. Landes, Trans.). London, England: Routledge. (Original work published 1945)

Middendorf, I. (1995). Interview with Ilse Middendorf. In H. Johnson (Ed.), *Bone, breath, and gesture: Practices of embodiment* (pp. 67–79). Berkeley, CA: North Atlantic Books.

Mohr, C., Rohrenbach, C. M., Landis, T., & Regard, M. (2001). Associations to smell are more pleasant than to sound. *Journal of Clinical and Experimental Neuropsychology, 23*(4), 484–489.

Moore, T. (1989). Introduction. In J. Hillman, *A blue fire* (p. 15). New York, NY: Harper & Row.

Palmer, R. (1969). *Hermeneutics: Interpretation theory in Schleiermacher, Dilthey, Heidegger, and Gadamer.* Evanston, IL: Northwestern University Press.

Plailly, J., Howard, J. D., Gitelman, D. R., & Gottfried, J. A. (2008). Attention to odor modulates thalamocortical connectivity in the human brain. *The Journal of Neuroscience, 28*(20), 5257–5267.

Porteous, D. J. (1985). Smellscape. *Progress in physical geography, 9*(3), 356–378.

Porteous, D. J. (1996). *Environmental aesthetics: Ideas, politics, and planning.* New York, NY: Routledge.

Psyche. (1997). In *The Oxford pocket dictionary and thesaurus* (American ed.). New York, NY: Oxford University Press.

Psychology. (1997). In *The Oxford pocket dictionary and thesaurus* (American ed.). New York, NY: Oxford University Press.

Reid, C., Green, J. D., Wildschut, T., & Sedikides, C. (2015). Scent-evoked nostalgia. *Memory, 23*(2), 157–166.

Ricoeur, P. (1981). *Hermeneutics and the human sciences* (J. Thompson, Trans.). New York, NY: Cambridge University Press.

Rilke, R. M. (2011). *Auguste Rodin.* New York, NY: Parkstone International.

Rindisbacher, H. J. (2015). What's this smell? *KulturPoetik, 15*(1), 70–104.

Rodaway, P. (1994). *Sensuous geographies: Body, sense, and place.* New York, NY: Routledge.

Routledge, C., Hart, C., Vingerhoets, A., Arndt, J., Juhl, J., & Schlotz, W. (2011). The past makes the present meaningful: Nostalgia as an existential resource. *Journal of Personality and Social Psychology, 101*(3), 638–652.

Rowland, S. (2010). *Taking the soul's path: C. G. Jung in the humanities.* New Orleans, LA: Spring Journal Books.

Royet, J. P., Martin, C. D., & Plailly, J. (2013). Odor mental imagery in non-experts in odors: A paradox? *Frontiers in Human Neuroscience, 7*(87), 1–6.

Saive, A. L., Royet, J. P., & Plailly, J. (2014). A review on the neural bases of episodic odor memory: From laboratory-based to autobiographical approaches. *Frontiers in Behavioral Neuroscience, 8*, 1–13.

Schacter, D., Gilbert, D., Wegner, D., & Nock, M. (2015). *Introducing psychology* (3rd ed.). New York, NY: Worth Publishers.

Schopenhauer, A. (2010). *The world as will and representation.* Cambridge, England: Cambridge University Press.

Sensation. (1997). *The Oxford pocket dictionary and thesaurus* (p. 725, American ed.). New York, NY: Oxford University Press.

Shamdasani, S., & Hillman, J. (2013). *Lament of the dead.* New York, NY: W. W. Norton and Company.

Soul. (1997). In *The Oxford pocket dictionary and thesaurus* (American ed.). New York, NY: Oxford University Press.

Sperber, D. (1975). *Rethinking symbolism.* Cambridge, England: Cambridge University Press.

Stein, M. (2015). *Jung's map of the soul: An introduction.* Chicago, IL: Open Court: Carus Publishing Company.

Toffolo, M. B. J., Smeets, M. A. M., & van den Hout, M.A. (2012). Proust revisited: Odours as triggers of aversive memories. *Cognition and Emotion, 26*(1), 83–92.

Tolstoy, L. (2007). *War and peace* (R. Pevear & L. Volokhonsky, Trans.) New York, NY: Vintage.

Wheelwright, P. (1959). *Heraclitus.* New Delhi, India: Isha Books.

Woodman, M. (1984). Psyche/soma awareness. *Quadrant, 17*(2), 25–37.

Woodman, M. (1993). *Conscious femininity: Interviews with Marion Woodman.* Toronto, Canada: Inner City Books.

Zola, E. (2000). *L'Assommoir* [The Dram Shop] (R. Buss, Trans.). London, England: Penguin Books.